giuseppe di giovanni

AGRIGENTO

an archeological itinerary

THE VALLEY OF THE TEMPLES
THE NATIONAL ARCHEOLOGICAL MUSEUM

By the same author:

* Akragas fra mito e storia - Agrigento
* Naro - Itinerario archeologico - Agrigento
* La città dei Dioscuri - Agrigento
* La Comunità Montana della Quisquina - S. Giovanni Gemini (AG)
* Siracusa - Monumenti e musei - S. Cataldo (CL)
* Agrigento araba - Agrigento
* Raffadali nel suo ambiente antico ed attuale - Agrigento
* Piazza Armerina - La civiltà romana attraverso i mosaici della Villa del Casale - Agrigento
* Il Polo turistico di Sciacca - Agrigento
* Selinunte - Testimonianze di un popolo - Agrigento
* Casteltermini - La Sagra del Tataratà - Agrigento
* Agrigento, città greca: governi, economia e forme di vita - Agrigento

☐ Culture prize of the Presidency of the Council of Ministers
☐ Telamone prize
☐ « Targa della Concordia » - National prize

• Member of the Società Siciliana per la Storia Patria - Palermo

The drawings were made by: Davide La Mendola, Franco Vitellaro, Tony Pecoraro, Hendrike Schoof, Yoseph Bonfante, G. Walnofer, G. Paltinger, S. Magro, Emanuele Puma, Massimo Di Piazza, Sabrina Gaetani, Giuseppe Rizzo, Michele Punturo, Basilio Borgo.

The choice of colours was made by: Franz La Paglia, Giovanni Bellavia, Franco Cremone, Nino Sciangula, Giosuè Arnone, Filippo Abissi, Giuseppe Bruccoleri, Roberto Meli, Giulio Montalbano, Cartolibreria G. Di Leo, Guglielmo Trapani, Filippo Tarallo.

This book was conceived by the author who welcomes any advice or comment. His adress is: **Via Salita S. Giacomo, 15 - 92100 Agrigento.**

Translation by Giovanna Lombardo.

Stampa: **SICULgrafica scarl** - Villaggio Mosé (AG)

PREFACE

This itinerary aims to rise one's own interest to know the mythical "Valley of the temples" dotted with doric monuments. It is an invitation to visit the famous masterpieces which represent the wonderful world of the Siceliot civilization.

The most secret and inner part is represented by the works that one can see in the National Museum: relics of even small sizes evoke the beauties of an advanced civilization, its myths, its legends and the passions of those who lived in that particular artistic, cultural and prosperous atmosphere that produced a way of living which made this land an extremely interesting country.

A very ancient land associates very prestigious monuments with a charm that in spite of all vicissitudes still conquers nowadays like in the past all those who have the privilege of visiting it; this land captivated Empedocles and charmed Pindar who acclaimed it as "the most beautiful of the mortal cities".

This book that was not designed for specialists aims to be a pleasant and informative guide to the classical ruins.

I would like to thank Archeologist Pr. Ernesto de Miro, Head of the Soprintendenza alle Antichità for Agrigento, who has carried out a research about the Rhodian and Cretan penetration in the Agrigento hinterland. His researches, in spite of the limited available means, have produced some great results: Mount Adranone, Mount Saraceno, Sabaucina, Vassallaggi, Morgantina are not covered with the fog of the past any more.

Because of the great amount of finds it is needed to arrange new local museums. One of them, the museum of Caltanissetta in close to be realized. Moreover a new room dedicated to Luigi Preti (the sixteenth room) will be opened in the National Museum of Agrigento.

The objects that come from the above mentioned sites will be contained in five glass-cases and thanks to Dr. Graziella Fiorentini, director of the museum and Assistant of the Soprintendenza Archeologica for Agrigento, they will be desplayed in a cronological, environmental and artistic order.

Because of the increasing richness and importance of its collections, the Museum of Agrigento is the favourite destination of those who consider both science and art as their "raison d'etre".

I wish to thank Pr. Filippo Tornambè, Avv. Giuseppe Grillo, Pr. Antonio Palermo, Pr. Anselmo Prado, Mgr. Angelo Ginex, Gerlando Bianchini, Dr. Settimio Biondi and Dr. Luigi Peritore, director of the Public tourist Organization for Agrigento, for their suggestions and advices.

Last but not least I thank the staff of the Sopreintendenza Archeologica for Agrigento for their hospitality and firm courtesy.

Giuseppe di Giovanni

3

A BRIEF HISTORICAL OUTLINE

Since the discovery of the Emporium at the mouth of the river Agrakas, it has been proved that the foundation of the town was preceded with a trading settlement not far from the mouth of the river that according to Elianus gave the name to the town.

What was in the very distant past only a village of which we do not know the name, later became one of the biggest cities of the Mediterranean coast, where according to Cicero « the clear sky doesn't know sunless day »: the Greek Akragas, the Roman Agrigentum, the Arabic Kerkent where the name of Girgenti comes from, today's Agrigento. It was founded in 581 B.C. on the most geographically useful site of the Mediterranean coast by Rhodian and Cretan colonists.

According to tradition Aristinoo and Pistilo were its founders. The topography of the area was particulary favourable to profitable trading with the near and rich Carthago, the soil was fertile for human needs. Needs and fulfilments were naturally balanced. Hence the town reached according to Pindar an amazing wealth as it is shown by its temples, its perstyles, its statues and its works of art.

Here the Greek genius found all the elements for producing masterpieces and for reaching a development that no future generations would reach again. On the other hand, not even the whole world willl ever produce again a population as harmoniously civilized as the one which moved to the Mediterranean coasts 26 centuries ago.

The clear sky, the calm landscape with clear-cut outlines, and the shape and colours of this land certainly formed the artistic taste of its inhabitants.

The town lies on a slight slope down to the sea, only three miles away. Rivers flow to the East and to the West of this Valley: the Akragas river is the today's S. Biagio and the Hipsas today is called Drago.

They circumscribe the perimeter of the town on two sides and to the South of its walls the Hipsas joins the Akragas and ends up in the sea.

The layout of the ancient town looked like a naturally fortified amphitheatre, boarded with two hills: Girgenti Hill and the Rupe Atenea that is 351 m. above the sea level.

The defences of the town were its natural highlands and a labirynth of gorges and hollows. The urban area covered 456 hectares and it was surrounded by a 12.90 Km. long wall that had 9 gates among which the « V » shaped one or the Holy Gate - that is the so called Scea and Dipilon Gate (with double gateways) - represent a very interesting kind of fortification and an example of the military building technique of that time. According to Politi and to Pardi the population consisted of 600,000 inhabitants, while from Laertius' point of view there lived 800,000 people, and from Beloch's standpoint there lived only 200,000 people.

Several famous and illustrious people spent some time in Agrigento as it was one of the most important towns and even if it never became as powerful as Syracuse, it was as rich, as voluptuous, cultivated and civilized.

The outstanding figure of the first period was Tyrant Phalaris (570-554 B.C.) who governed successfully both from the political and from the military point of view. He increased the political influence of the town , he wanted its walls to be built, he extended Agrigento territory which stretched from Termini Imerese to Lentini and according to Suida he invented new war machines and conquered Sicanian and Greek towns.

It was the time of Stesicoro, of Pitagora and of doctor Policleto from Messina who became famous for having treated the tyrant Phalaris of a very serious disease while the people wished him to die.

Phalaris is famous because of the legend of the bronze bull made by the Athenian sculptor Perillo inside which the tyrant roasted his enemies alive. This work was made so well that the screams of the victim reproduced the roars of a true bull.

In about 554 B.C. he died a death that was as violent as his behaviour had been: he was stoned by the inhabitants of Agrigento, a town he had made rich, populous and powerful in 16 years.

This tyrant was so much hated that the new Government of Agrigento firmly ordered not to wear blue clothes as this had been the favourite colour of the tyrant.

However, Agrigento became both an active centre of the Mediterranean culture and a great military power with the tyrant Theron (488-472 B.C.). Indeed the short beautiful period of prosperity of Sicily started after the victory over the mercenaries that Carthago had gathered from all the Mediterranean coasts, who were defeated near Himera (today's Termini Imerese) in 480 B.C.. The victory of Himera produced the greatest results in the political, economic and religious fields.

The power and the prestige of Agrigento grew: it shared 2,000 talents with Syracuse; it took other 1,600 talents from carthaginian prisoners and it forced the Carthaginians to carry out human sacrifices during worships. Montesquieu mentions this treaty as the first and the best in the history of mankind.

Agrigentans managed to capture the highest number of carthaginian prisoners and several citizens obtained even 500 of them each.

However most slaves were used for building the temples and the underground canals of the town, for draining the marshes and building the port; these works were planned by the famous architect Feace and by Empedocles.

Then Pindar wrote an olimpic ode in honour of the victory of Theron's quadriga at the LXXVI Olimpic Games (474 B.C.) and the following mystical line (ol. 111): "Akragas, the most beatiful City the mortals had ever built".

According to tradition, the Cavoline ravine that is better known as the Empedocles' ship which devides the two hills (the Girgenti Hill and the Rupe Atenea) that is between the today's Roma Square and Vittorio Emanuele Square, was planned by Empedocles.

Diodorus Siculus says that the great philosopher who was very skilled in medicine and public health suggested that cut in order to let the north wind into the valley of the town thus draining the marshes and defeated malaria. Theron's time was the golden age of Agrigento. The art of tragedy, an original greek creation, developed in the town with Calcino and Callicratide, an Empedocles' brother.

It was the time of philosopher Polo, a Gorgia's disciple, of Evemero who tried to set back the religion of the Greeks and was prosecuted and banned from all towns as a consequence of that. It was the time of Empedocles, the philosopher of the theory of soul transmigration, who discovered in himself the soul of a fish as he was able to swim perfectly, the soul of a bird as he was able to be as fast as an arrow and like Pitagor the soul of a God. He used to walk around the town wearing a red cloak embroidered in gold and a circle of leaves of laurel around his curly long hair. Everywhere, thousands of people beseeched him to cure them of their disease, to tell them about their future and they followed him as they hoped to witness some miracles. Very rarely, a philosopher was so much praised by his disciples as Empedocles who started to be venerated almost like a God after he died. He had refused the royal crown the citizens of Agrigento had offered him after an insurrection.

It was the time of historian Philino who wrote about the first Punic War; he was nicknamed the little Thucydides.

Medicine was one of the Agrigentans' favourite science and other doctors are mentioned besides Empedocles: Acrone, a friend of his, who was famous for having defeated the plague in Athens,

The tyrant Phalaris gets stoned by the Agrigentans.

7

and Pausania, his rival, who wrote a treatise on diet; when Plato came to Sicily, as a pedagogue of Dionysius the 2nd, he said: « all chief cooks must leave the town ». However, nobody listened to him: too rich and too refined banquets carried on taking place during parties.

Moderate democracy introduced by Empedocles lasted for a long time. However, the citizens' habits became very similar to those of Sibari's: people became very lazy as they were rich and everybody complained everytime they were uncomfortable. In order to give you an idea of that time it is enough to mention that when the town was besieged by the Carthaginians it was ordered

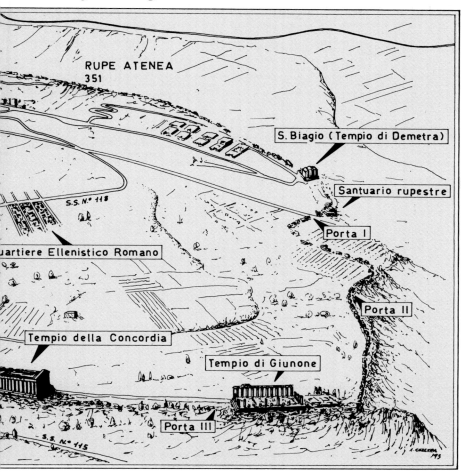

that none of the guards who spent the nights at their posts should have more than one mattress, one cover and two pillows. Such great wealth is also shown by magnificent private buildings: the house with the perystile in the Hellenistic and Roman Quarter looks like it was built for loose and rich living. This magnificent house consists of 42 rooms. It is inserted in a grid plan known to be concieved by philosopher Hippodamos from Mileto who lived in the 5th century B.C.. This building covers a 1,850 mq. area which is as big as ten apartments of 185 mq. each, that to-day are considered as wealthy.

Empedocles used to say that « the Akragantines ate as if they would die tomorrow, while they built as if they would live forever ».

When Esseneto won the quadriga race in 416 B.C., he was borne in triumph around the streets of the town and at least 300 chariots drawn by two white horses each, followed him.

The wealth of some citizens like Antistene and Gellias was amazing: Antistene invited all citizens to his daughter's wedding: the bridal procession consisted of almost 800 bigas (two-horse chariot) and of a host of horsemen. Moreover, her father wanted all altars of the temples to be covered with faggots that were all burned at once after a particular signal was given from the Rupe Atenea.

Gellia was even wealthier than Antistene. In his cellars he had 300 barrels cut into the rock which had a capacity of 100 amphorae each. Besides these cellars he had a masonry cistern that had a capacity of 1,000 amphorae from which the wine flowed into vases. 31,000 wine vases were filled with 840,060,000 litres (a Roman amphora contained 26.26 liters), that was the content of his cellars. Gellias owned a 145 hectare vineyard that needed a staff of 75 people.

Diodorus said that once Gellias, who used to post some of his servants by the gates of the town in order to invite all strangers to get an accomodation in his hotels, was able to give lodgings to 500 horsemen caught in a violent storm on their way to Gela. He also gave them a change of clothes making to each a present of a himation and a chiton which represented the Greeks' main clothes. All this gives us an idea about the magnificence of their houses, their wealth and the elegance of their banquets, too.

Akragas remained neutral in the war between Athens and Syracuse in 413 B.C.. But shortly after, the very beautiful town that was described as « big » by Empedocle, as « wide » by Plinius and as « very opulent » by Diodorus Siculus, was besieged in the Spring of 406 B.C. by the Carthaginians. For eight months the siege dragged on. Finally, after the mercenary troops of Desippus and Dafneo gave up, the town was taken and completely destroyed. It was left abandonend till Timoleon beat the Carthaginians in the battle of the Crimiso river (today's Belice river) in 340 B.C. and rebuilt the town. He brought new colonists from the mother-country. The past wealth revived in Timoleon's Akragas thanks to the colonists from Elea and to their leaders Pheristos and Maegellus in 339 B.C.. Timoleon gave the Akragantines a democratic Constitution.

Then the destiny of both Agrigento and Sicily will be tied to the more turbulent and long history of ancient Rome.

In 210 B.C. Lavinius Consul who succeeded Marcellus besieged Agrigento and after he took the town thanks to a clever diplomatic move, he allowed his troops to sack it.

According to historians Amico and Narbone, soon after that Titus Manlius, Praetor of Sicily, complying with an order of the Roman Senate, gathered those who lived in the serroundings and founded a new colony in 208 B.C..

Agrigento like the whole island became the granary of Rome, and was classified as « decumana »: it had to give Rome 20% of its crops.

As soon as Rome declined the town had to deal both with the Byzantines and with the Arabs who firstly destroyed it completely in 828 and then reconstructed it on the top of Girgenti Hill.

The Arabs were followed by the Normans who besieged the town on April the Ist in 1087, burned the fields and managed to control the inhabitants' supplies. Hunger compelled the Agrigentans to live on human corpses. After a resistance that started on July the 25th in 1087 and dragged on for 116 days, the gates were opened and the town surrendered to the Normans. That was how Agrigento after 259 years of Arab rule was given back to Christianity by Count Roger.

The Normans were followed by the Swabians, the Spanish and the Burbons.

Today, the district of Agrigento consists of 43 Comunes where there lived in 1971 447,271 people (49,293 in Agrigento only), that is 9.6% of the regional population.

Here the weather is typical mediterranean: heavy rain during the Winter and long hot Summers. Two islands: Lampedusa and Linosa, only 113 Km. away from the Tunisian coast and 215 Km. away from the Agrigento one, close the topographical geography of the district area. This very ancient land with a glorious but at the same time hard past and with a difficult present, still charmes today all those who have the chance to visit it.

This enchanted land: 25 centuries ago when the protagonists of its history were Empedocles, Theron, Hannibal, Philinius, Mida, Gellias, Esseneto; last century when they were Goethe and Amari; and this century with Huesse, President of the Republic of Germany, Guido Pioveni, Luigi Pirandello who asked for his ashes to be placed facing the African sea inside a rough stone.

11

CHURCH OF SAINT NICHOLAS

The church of Saint Nicholas is the building which dominates the Valley of the temples. From there you can enjoy the view of the Doric temples which become even more charming when sunsets paint them gold. With a simple and grand facade, a nice ogival doorway and a touching austere interior hermetically sealed in its warm sandstone cover, the church of Saint Nicholas represents one of the best examples of Gothic and Cistercian architecture.

It has a rectangular plan and a nave covered with an ogival vault. To the right of the nave there are four chapels where the

Cistercian monks used to pray on their own. In one of them you can see the famous sarcophagus that evokes the myth of Phoedra and Hyppolitus.

On eight blind arches on the long sides and on five more on one of the short sides, there are some frescoes that were made later (1575) by painter Innocenzo Mascarella. The big wooden door was made by Angelo Blundo (1531).

The church, built during the 12th century, was given to the Cistercians of Santa Maria of Adrano by Bishop Ugone in 1219. It was restored and modified in 1430 thanks to Bishop Matteo Cimarra.

An old wooden Cross is venerated in this church. It is the so called « Christ of the Ship » and his feast celebrated on September the Ist inspired Luigi Pirandello who wrote about it.

THE SARCOPHAGUS OF PHOEDRA

A sarcophagus stands in the middle of the second chapel of the church of St. Nicholas. This is the famous sarcophagus of Phoedra that Goethe mentions as « one of most elegant examples of Greek art ». It seems that movement, originality, realism and powerful creativity have reached in this sculpture the highest way of expression.

It is made of white marble.

The long sides are 2.28 m. by 1.19 m., while the short sides are 1.08 m. by 1.19 m..

This sarcophagus that dates back to about the 3rd century A.D., was found in the 18th century. It is very richly ornamented and evokes the myth of Phoedra and Hyppolitus on its four sides.

On the western long side, Hyppolitus is depicted as leaving for a hunt. He wears a chlamys that is a short cloak and he is surrounded by ten hunters, dogs, and horses; on his right, his wet nurse is giving him Phoedra's love message humbly trying to convince him to accept it. Hyppolitus rejects the message scornfully, but at the same time he keeps it to himself.

The southern side represents Phoedra who has just been rejected by Hyppolitus. She has just dropped on a stool, her head is turned towards the wet nurse who is lifting her veil up and unplainting her hair. At the same time nine of her maids are tenderly trying to be as close to her as possible and to confort her by singing and playing the lyra.

The other long side that was left unfinished represents a wild boar hunting scene that is taking place in a pine wood. Hyppolitus who is riding a beautiful horse is going to strike with his lance a frightened wild boar that is surrounded by five dogs. Three hunters armed with a club, a stone and an arrow are trying to kill it. At the same time a fifth character is provoking with his right hand a dog that is biting one of the back legs of the wild boar, while in his left hand he is holding a sword.

The fourth side of the sarcophagus that is the least sculptured one, shows the dramatic death of Hyppolitus. He has just fallen from his charriot and three frisky horses are dragging him. They got frigtened as soon as they saw a scaly sea monster. A proud slave is trying with difficulty to stop them by holding their bridles. Hyppolitus who has been thrown on a rock is lifeless. The head of a hornless bull can be seen on the left side.

THE EKKLESIASTERION

The Ekklesiasterion or Comitium was the place where those citizens who had full rights used to meet in order to discuss the affairs of the State every nine days.

A religious ceremony that consisted of sacrificing either a calf or a pig to Zeus opened all sessions at dawn. Then the President started to read the orders of the day. Then the discourse started and the oldest always spoke first. Those who proposed a particular law were responsible for it. Indeed, if it failed, it was abolished within a year and its proposer was fined.

Usually they voted by show of hands. However, ballots were needed sometimes, too. With regard to meetings the attendance of a great number of people was not required except for those days when an ostracism had to take place, that was a judicial procedure for banishing a citizen from the town.

Every year at the start of Spring, citizens were asked if they wished to banish someone for ten years. Those who wished to, had to write those people's names on a shard (the « ostraka »): the « winner » was compelled to leave the town; obviously this was a precautionary measure against any attempt of tyranny.

Ostracism was firstly introduced by Clistene in 508 B.C. and fell into disuse at the end of the Vth century.

All those citizens who attended meetings and did not go to work received an attendance check that was the so called « moskos ekklesiaskos ».

Orators used to speak either from the orchestra or from a rounded flat area in the middle, where there was an altar for sacrifices that was always used at the beginning of meetings.

The Ekklesasterion could contain almost 3,000 people who used to sit on 22 rows of horizontal seats that were vertically devided into five sections. The cavea is 18 m. wide, while the radius of the orchestra is 7 m. long. The Ekklesasterion was built in the IVth century B.C.

THE SO CALLED ORATORY OF PHALARIS

The name of the Oratory of Phalaris comes from a legend according to which in that spot there used to stand the palace of Phalaris. Actually it is a Hellenistic in antis building where the cast front consisted of four Ionic columns supporting a Doric trabeation. The temple dates back to about the IInd century B.C. and was structurally restored by the Goths who adapted it to their style. They made some ogival arches on the outside walls and a cross vault inside. This temple is 10.50 m. long and 7.30 m. wide.

TEMPLE OF HERA LACINIA

In the grand temple of Hera Lacinia, who the Romans called Juno, newly wed couples, after a purifying bath in the river Agrakas, used to offer Hera Pronuba, the protector of marriage, as a symbol of their lasting love, a female lamb that had both its bile and its other entrails removed.

According to Plutarco, before the sacrifice started they threw

THE ORATORY OF PHALARIS

This temple reminds of the legend of the cruel tyrant of Agrigento (from 570 to 554 B.C.) who required Perillo to build a hollowed bronze bull inside which he put his ennemies and then made the statue red-hot. The victims' screams sounded outside like natural roars of a real bull.

some cold water on it: if that animal reacted the ceremony was delayed. The bride used to wear a sleeveless white tunic that covered her feet, too. She had a belt tied around her waist that was the so called « Erakles' knot ».

At the end of the sacrifice a priest took the bride's and the groom's right hands and put them one over the other. This was the most solemn part of the wedding: they both promised to live happily together.

Racing competitions for women only during the feasts of Juno

More than any other people, the Greeks believed in the motto "healthy mind healthy body" they were therefore the happiest and most harmonious people on earth. There were no Greek cities without a public "gymnasium" with vast fields exposed to the sun, fenced in by columns or rows of trees. School were called "ginnasi"* from the word 'gumnòs' meaning 'nude', due to the fact that the exercising was actually done whilst nude; thus the word "gymnastics". During these solemn feasts the people gathered to watch the games, thus gymnastics became part of the religion. Only during the feasts of Juno were the competitions reserved to the women only.

According to Pausania these games were reserved to women only because they were the promotors and the protagonists of these feasts in honour of the goddess Juno.

Every five years, infact, sixteen virgins weaved a cloak and offered it to the goddess; after which the races commenced. The young women belonged to different age groups: the youngest girls were the first to compete, followed by women a little older and lastly the oldest. When the competitions finished, the winners, with the crowd of friends and relatives, went merrily to the temple of Juno, and it was here, at the feet of the goddess, that the judges sat, they then bestowed the prizes upon the winners; here was also the sacred table, with freshly cut olive crowns. In the sight of the goddess the winners were crowned. The winner was also given part of the meat consacrated to Juno during the sacrifice and the right to present a painting of herself to the goddess.

N. B. The word "ginnasi" in the Italian language means "high schools".

Sometime later the married couple came back to this temple for thanking the Goddess. This ceremony consisted of offering the Goddess the bride's belt that was too tight as she got pragnant.

The Erakles' knot had to be undone by her husband in front of their friends. The ceremony was at the same time very colourful, solemn and lively: fire and smoke arose to the clear sky; choral songs and flutes accompanied the ceremony.

However, this temple was the sanctuary of those Agrigentan married women whose husbands were unfaithful. They used to come here to share silently their destiny with Jupiter's wife whose marriage was often characterized by arguments because of the God's several love stories. Poets mention Hera as the symbol of both conjugal bond and woman's fidelity.

All mythology and especially the poets' literary one was symbolic as for example Hera, by marrying Jupiter, became the Queen of the sky. The sky is not always clear: often there are violent storms and in the Winter it is almost constantly cloudy. Such weather disturbances symbolized the arguments of the divine married couple. However, only a breath of wind is enough to clear the sky as well as only a smile is enough to restore peace and love between a husband and his wife. The fact that the blue sky of Agrigento is one of the nicest ones means that this was the Goddess favourite site.

The present name of this temple is as traditional as those of the other monuments of Agrigento. However, it is nice to report the following interesting story that Pliny, Diodorus and Aristotle mentioned in their works.

Zeusi was ordered to paint a portrait of Helen. The most beautiful woman of antinquity was born from an egg that Leda had conceived with Zeus who had turned himself into a swan. This portrait had to be painted for the temple of Hera the Goddess of fertility who presided over births and protected marriage. The painter accepted, but at the same time he asked for the five most beautiful girls of the town to pose naked for him as he needed to choose the most beautiful one. The town agreed and all girls competed for being chosen. With regard to Zeusi's Helen, Beloch says: « For the first time he gave it a natural expression ».

The painting revealed to all those who saw it a new magic world. It is said that as there were too many people who wanted

to see it, the painter decided to ask them to pay to see it. Moreover, it is said that he managed to make quite a lot of money, too ».

However, Cicero and Dyonisus from Alicarnasso report this episode as it had taken place in Crotone. As a matter of fact in that town there was a temple dedicated to the same Goddess. Moreover, Zeusi had spent a long time after he had lost to his rival Parrasios in Athens.

As there is no evidece for the name of this temple, let's analyse it from the technical point of view.

The architetture of this temple that stands on the East of the Valley of the Temples, 120 m. on the sea level, reveals the effort to produce artistic perfection.

The interior is surrounded by a colonnade and consists of three rooms: the pronaos, the cella and the opisthodomos. On a four step pedestal at the bottom of the cella there used to stand the statue representing the divinity.

On each side of the entrance which is 3.23 m. wide, there were two winding staircases giving access to the roof space. This building, that like all the others faces East, has a considerable size: the rectangular stylobate that stands on the top of four high steps and that supports 34 columns (six of them stand to the front while 13 more stand on each side) is 41.106 m. by. 20.260 m.: it has the shape of two squares and covers in area of 832.807 mq.. This area is seven and a half time smaller than the area covered by the temple of Olympian Zeus. The temple of Hera

was 15.31 m. high.

Its columns consist of four drums and have 20 flutes each separated by sharp edges: they are 6.32 m. high and their base diameter is 1.70 m. The distance between the middle columns is 1.76 m. while the distance between the side columns is 1.71 m..

This is the style of the Greek classical period, thus this temple is dated about 450-440 B.C. It became a national monument in 1748. Today 30 columns are standing and only 16 of them have still got their capitals. At the time of Historian Tommaso Fazello (1490-1570) this building was intact. It was restored in 1787 by Torremuzza. The stains of fire that can still be seen on the walls of the cella prove the pillage by the Carthagininans in 406 B.C. when they destroyed the town completely.

The Greek Wedding

The picture illustrates a wedding cerimony. The bride is on the chariot, between the bridegroom and the paranymph, who had also arranged the marriage from an economical point of view. She is wearing a long, white peplum, with train and veil. The numerous guest all wear new clothes for the occasion (often it was the bride's family who presented the less richer guests with new and luxurious clothes). The wedding took place with all the proper solemnities and publicity as there were no public records regarding civil state, only the people present could give evidence as to whether the union was legal. The family, proud of their wealth, showed all the wedding presents to the guests. The Greek wedding, of course,was a religious solemnity, as was the wedding feast. The engagement itself had already been perfomed before the alter, with a solemn promise from the bride's father to give his daughter in wife to the fiancè. The propitiatory sacrifices and the rites ended, the priest then took the right hand of the bride and groom, placing one on top of the other, this was the most solemn moment of the wedding, in which, the bride and groom vowed to live together, in happiness, forever. The husband then laced the bride's belt of virginity (Hercules Knot; hence the word "incinta"* used to describe a woman with child who, because of her pregnancy, could not wear the belt too tight around the waist). The people present then threw wheat, barley and pomegranite, in the hope that the couple may have many children. Choir singing and music accompanied the cerimony which ended with a banquet, offered by the bride's parents, in honour of the guests and the gods. Undoubtedly the weddings of today have much in common with the Greek weddings: the long, white wedding dress; the wide veil; the holding of hands; the banquet; the new clothes of the wedding guests; the bride being carried over the threshold of the new home so as not to touch it; the wedding ring, which, according to Aulo Gellio was worn (at it is today) on the annular finger, because it was believed that a very fine nerve went from this finger straight to the heart. Also, the expression "to ask for the bride's hand in mariage", comes from the word "manu" due to the fact the it was imposition of hands that symbolized the assumption of authority.

* In the Italian languge the words "incinta" and "mano" mean pregnant and hand.

23

This drawing is by Hendrike Schoof and Abel Escobar.

The Temple of Juno Lacinia rises amid a sparse growth of millenary olive trees.

By Philip Hackert, 1785 - The author of this water colour picture said that only the Valley of the Temples evoked in himself a deeply harmonious atmosphere more than any other classical site.

GREEK MARRIAGE

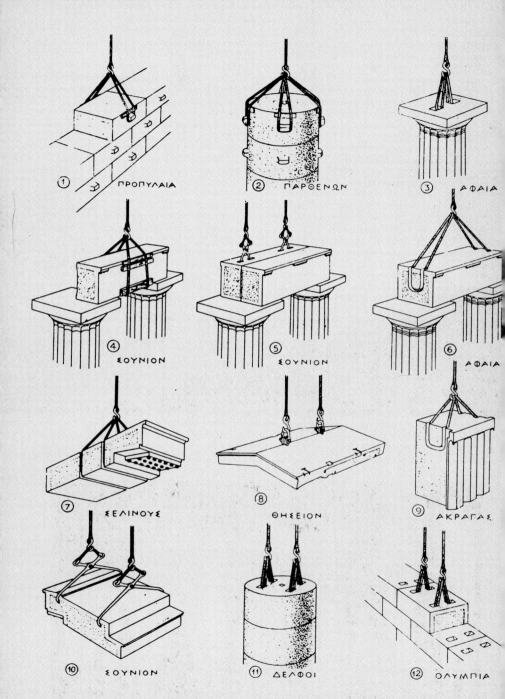

1. ΠΡΟΠΥΛΑΙΑ
2. ΠΑΡΘΕΝΩΝ
3. ΑΦΑΙΑ
4. ΣΟΥΝΙΟΝ
5. ΣΟΥΝΙΟΝ
6. ΑΦΑΙΑ
7. ΣΕΛΙΝΟΥΣ
8. ΘΗΣΕΙΟΝ
9. ΑΚΡΑΓΑΣ
10. ΣΟΥΝΙΟΝ
11. ΔΕΛΦΟΙ
12. ΟΛΥΜΠΙΑ

An example of dry assembling the different parts of a building which are marked with greek letters.

TEMPLE OF CONCORD

The view of this temple inserted in this incomparable scenery characterized by a clear blue sky where the sun always shines is unique in the world. Indeed, anyone who watches this precious example of ancient Hellenic grandeur with its fine elegant doric features, admires it as one of the greatest and most significant expressions of the Greek genius.

Linear outlines, perfectly balanced features, total harmony, an imposing effect that can only be understood from a close proximity, changeable golden tones of its warm sandstone. In other words everything makes it one of the most admirable monuments that can be seen. It inspires both meditation and wonder and it proves that even in Agrigento the Greeks included the sense of infinity and mistery in the idea of perfection.

What precision and clearness! Ratios are simple and proportions are perfect. The architecture of this building, that dates back to about 430 B.C., is the typical Greek one. It is 19.758 m. by 42.230 m.: it is a bit bigger than a double square. It covers an area of 843.38 mq. and it is 13.481 m. high.

Because of its shape, the pediment has been compared to an

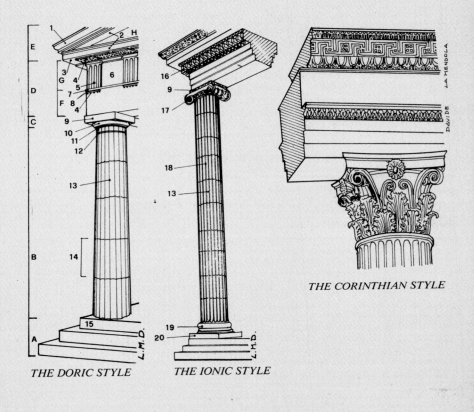

THE DORIC STYLE

THE IONIC STYLE

THE CORINTHIAN STYLE

A - Steps	1 - Sima	11 - Rings
B - Shaft	2 - Cornice	12 - Astragalus
C - Capital	3 - Mutule	13 - Fluting
D - Trabeation	4 - Drips	14 - Drum
E - Horizontal cornice	5 - Triglyph	15 - Stylobate
	6 - Metope	16 - Dentil
F - Architrave	7 - Taenia	17 - Volute
G - Frieze	8 - Regula	18 - Flat
H - Pediment	9 - Aabacus	19 - Torus
	10 - Echinus	20 - Plinth

The doric and ionic columns were born nearly in the meantime (VII cent) while the Corinthian order appeared later (V cent.), Vitruvio tells Dorics saw human foot is equal to a sixth of his height, and transferred this relation to their columns, giving so them the same harmony of a human body, the ionic column is more slender lighter and elegant. Vitruvio asserts, by an imaginotive comparison, the ionic column recalls, in the capital's volutes, the curly hair of woman, and the flutes recall the folds of a dress. The relation between the diameter and the column's height (1 to 8), unlike the doric one (1 to 6) take to the woman body, which is frailer than then man's one.

eagle with open wings. The lack of cramps and connections suggests that the pediment was not decorated. However, even the metopes lacked sculptures in relief. The raking trussed roof was covered with clay pan tiles that were fixed by simas. These were some kinds of gutters collecting rainwater and directing it towards the spouts that had the shape of lions' heads.

This temple, like all the others, faces East as according to both Greek and Roman religious rules the image of the God had to watch the sunrise which symbolized light and life, and never the sunset which symbolized night and death: the kingdom of Pluto was on the far West.

The present name of this temple was given by historian Tommaso Fazello (1490-1570) who found a Latin inscription nearby. However, there is no connection at all between that inscription and this building. In 597 this temple was turned into a Christian Basilica by Bishop Gregorio. He destroyed two pagan idols of the temple and as the name of one of them was Raps, the new church was dedicated to St. Gregorio delle Rape: twelve arcades

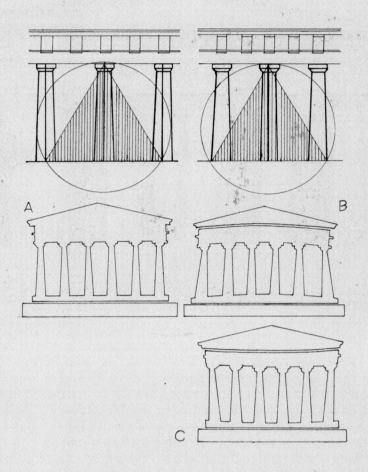

Drawing by Engineer Franco Vitellaro

Above: the proportions of the Greek temple are calculated according to an equilateral triangle (with its vertexes either on the axis of the columns or on the outside ends of the base diameter in order to obtain a more or less slender effect).
Below: examples of optical corrections. In order to make the temple A to look like temple C from a distance, it has to have the shape shown by temple B. As a matter of fact if it was built like picture A it would look like picture C from a distance.

were opened on the walls of the cella in order to obtain a Christian church with threee naves. The wall that used to devide the cella from the opisthodomos was knocked down and the intercolumnations, that is the spaces between the columns, were filled with dry-stone walls. Moreover, two niches were cut into the wall inside the cella: one of them can still be seen today. With regard to St. Gregorio who was born in the near village of Naro, his biographer Leontio says that as soon as he was named Bishop at the age of 31, he was sent to the Diocese of Agrigento. However, some citizens who supported somebody else accused him of having flirted with a woman. As consequence of that he was sent to Rome where after a long trial he was acquitted on the charge. It was the time of the law for celibacy that is mentioned by St. Girolamo at the end of the 4the century. As a matter of fact in 588, Pope Pelagio the 2nd ordered the Sicilian subdeacons to follow the law for celibacy and forbade them to get married.

On the other hand he ordered the already married ones to refrain from staying with their wives. The precept of Pelagio was stressed even more by Pope Gregory the 7th who defeated the debauchery of bishops, priests and archideacons: he decreed that all prelates' children who were born after the ordination of their fathers were condemned to hard labour.

From a technical point of view the building of a temple was planned and arranged in advance. The architect gave precise plans and measurements. *(Above)* The drawing shows the plan of a temple marked with measurements and with Greek letters over which they placed the already well cut corresponding parts.

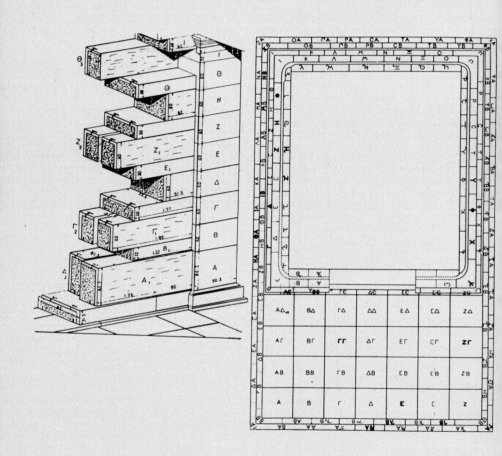

De Forbin, 1778 - A. Cellura, 1993.

This temple became national monument in 1743 and it was restored the same year by Torremuzza who knocked down the outside walls of the little normand church dedicated to St. Gregory which occupied the eastern part of the cella. Later in 1784 King Ferdinand visited the ancient monuments of Agrigento and ordered to knock down the remains of the small monastery built against the temple. He wanted the trabeation and the frieze to be restaured because of aesthetic reasons.

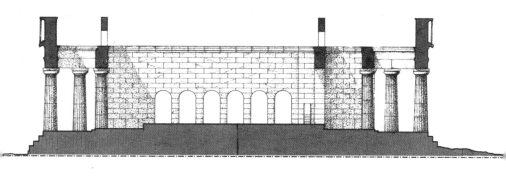

In 1767 Joseph Hermann, Baron of Riedesel said: " The temple of Concord allows visitors to understand the nice effect of noble simplicity and sober ornaments".

THE PALEOCHRISTIAN NECROPOLIS

The paleochristian cemetery is better know as the Fragapane Grotto and can be seen inside the the hypogees of Villa Aurea.
The funeral ceremony carried out in the cemeteries was burial: corpes covered with two sheets (« sudaria ») between which there was a layer of lime, were buried in the loculs which were cut into the sandstone walls of the tunnels leading to large rooms. Loculs were closed with slabs of the same stone. In some of the rocky chapels cut into the walls there are still some remains of religious paintings, while in some others there are some altars which are fundamental in the study of primitive Christianity.
The beautiful Villa Aurea was the last residece of the meritorious and singular British Captain Alex Hardcastle. He came to Agrigento in 1921, he moved to this villa and never wanted to leave it till he died in 1933 fully honoured by the town.

The average age of the adults was between 19 and 29; the death rate of babies was very high: 9 out of 12 children buried in a cemetery had died before the age of 10: the rate was 75%.

TEMPLE OF HERAKLES

Columns and ruins show visitors that today the temple of Herakles, one of the most beautiful of antiquity, is reduced to few poor remains. Even though, this building is imposing when seen from a distance. It stands in the Valley of the Temples as the symbol of Herakles' power and strength. He was the national hero of Sicily and Agrigento dedicated this somptuous temple to him and used to honour him by celebrating the Heraklean Feasts. Agrigentans used to invoke Herakles against the nightmares that occurred as deceptive dreams; it was wise to invoke him against sexual excitement in general and particularly at dawn when more violent sexual excitement occurred.

However, the hero who, according to Pindar had a small size and a hairy body, is better known for his legendary twelve labours: there is nothing more famous than Herakles in Greek mythology. He was the symbol of a young nation of warriors that was becoming more and more powerful, just like the Mycenean kingdom was the symbol of its moral strength.

He was aware of being brave: he set the world free from the lion of Nemea, a fierce monster that no armament could kill as it had an invulnerable skin. He killed the hydra of Lerna a

Building a temple without lime simply consisted of assembling already made dry parts, that were plastered and coloured afterwards. Working time corresponded to daylight. A drachma was the daily pay: it corresponds to today's 50,000 liras. According to the statement of accounts dating from 409-407 B.C., that refer to the building of the Eritteo, that is the temple of Athena and Poseidon, for the fluting of a column, 5 workers were paid 50 drachmae that is today's 4,500,000 liras. The bill for paying the artists who sculptured the frieze shows that the sculptors carved the different block individually. However, they managed to respect the same style

Arch. Calogero Palazzotto

From this document one can read that both the citizens, the metics and the slaves worked together in peace according to a fixed plan and for the same amount of money. 60 drachmae, that is today's 3,000,000 liras, paid the sculpture for a statue. The total cost of the frieze was 3,315 drachmae, that is 165,570,000 liras.

According to an inscription found in Athens and dating from about 414 B.C., the price of an adult slave was of 115-240 drachmae that is 6,750,000-11,000,000 liras; a baby slave costed 72 drachmae that is 3,600,000 liras.

water snake with nine heads that grew again everytime they were cut. He caught both the hind of Cerinea that had copper hooves and golden antlers and the fierce wild boar of Erimanto; he managed to clean the stables of Augia from the excrements of 3,000 oxen by making two rivers pass through them.

He exterminated with his arrows the Stinfalidi birds that had talons, beaks and wings made of bronze. They used their bronze feathers like arrows and fed on the humans and the animals they caught with them. He tamed the wild bull of Crete and killed Diomedes the King of Thrace, who fed his horses with human flesh: he defeated the Amazons the warlike women of Cappadocia who murdered the males and brought up the females only after having deprived them of their right breast so that they could use a bow. He stole the bulls of Geryon who had three bodies and owned a rich herd guarded by a seven-headed dragon and also by a two-headed dog; he got the golden apples that symbolized wealth from the Hesperides' garden where they were guarded by the dragon Ladones that had one hundred heads and was able

Vivant Denon said: " In this place the upside down capitals, the drums of columns, the plants, the movements of the plants and of the soil are mixed up in such an admirable way, that they make a great landscape.

44

to speak several languages; he took Theseus, the legendary hero of Attica, away from Hell and chained there the three-headed dog Cerberus.

Like the others, this temple faces East.

Its rectangular base that stands on four steps is 73.992 m. long and 27.788 m. wide. It reached a height of 16.264 m. Only 9 columns are left. Originally they were 38: 15 of them used to stand along each long side. They were reconstructed in 1922 thanks to the English Captain Hardcastle and today stand imposingly among the many ruins. The columns consisting of four sandstone drums have a diameter of 2.21 m. and are 10.00 m. high.

The cella was decorated with four columns and was 4.8 m. long and 13.00 m. wide. The horizontal cornice was decorated in red, pale blue and deep blue with meanders ending at the corners with upright palmettes and lion heads following the Greeks' architectural art of moulding of that time. The pediment was decorated with sculptures. A marble torso of a warrior was found in a cistern to the South of this temple. It reppresents one of the nicest Greek works of art attributed to Pitagora from Reggio and it can be seen in the third room of the National Museum.

THERON'S TOMB

An example of Roman art is the Heroon, or mausoleum dedicated to a dead hero. According to a popular tradition this is Theron's tomb. He governed the town from 488 B.C. to 472 B.C.. A new study believes it to be a mausoleum that the Romans built in honour of 30 thousand people who died during the siege of Agrigento in 262 B.C. It dates back to the first century B.C. and is a beautiful example of Doric and Ionic architecture.

It consists of a squared base of 5.20 m. wide and 3.90 m. high; it had a pyramidal shape and its upper part consists of a tower decorated with four Ionic columns with Doric capitals that on the corners were decorated with leaves and ovolos. On each side of the four walls there is a blind door in bas-relief. The columns are 3.35 m. high, while the building is 9.32 m. high.

TEMPLE OF ASKLEPIUS

It was here that sick and disabled peopel went.

Before entering the temple, pilgrims bathed in the clear water of the spring, then, they made the ritual sacrifices that often consisted of offering a cockerel to the God. Until a short time ago, people used to give that particular animal to the family doctor. The cockerel was the symbol of daylight and of waking in the Underworld. Before one's death a cockerel was usually sacrificed to Asklepius. Even Socrates asked for that just before he died. Asklepius was the God of goodness, son of Apollo and of the nymph Coronis. He had learned medicine from the centaur Chiron. His symbols were the sceptre, the crook and a roll of paper.

It is almost sure that the temple was dedicated to Asklepius; for the Romans he was Aesculapius. According to Polibius the building was eight stadiums and a half away from the town, that is 1,480 m. In the 4th book of the Verrine, Cicero said that this temple was a « famosisssimu fanum » that is a famous sanctuary, and he stated in the same book that in the temple there was a beautiful statue of Apollo made by Myron, the sculptor who was able to represent better than anybody else human beauty, its strength and vigour of movements. His name was written in silver letters on a thigh of the statue.

Apollo, the God of light and truth was highly venerated in Agrigento and the faithful came from all over in order to ask for his advice and his help, in order to know if it was worthy to get married or not, if they had to buy a new slave or if they could have children.

Heraclida wrote on a lead sheet: « Heraclida is asking God if he is going to have children from his present wife Egle ».

Representatives of villages and towns went there to ask this God about his will when they saw bad omens or if an epidemic occurred. The above mentioned statue was carried away by the Carthaginians when they sacked Agrigento in 406 B.C. Later it was given back to the town in 146 B.C. by Scipio the African and finally stolen by Verres.

The temple was built around 400-390 B.C.. It consisted of a cella in antis - that is with corner pillars - and of a pronaos with two columns standing on the same line of the pillars. On the western side there is a stairwell with four flights of stairs that used to reach the roof.

The temple of Asklepius was a very simple building: 22.144 m. long and 11.118 m. wide, covering a 246.196 mq. area. It was not as richly decorated as the classical Doric temples. The walls are 0.55 m. thick, while the diameter of the columns is 1.10 m. long.

ASKLEPIUS

The sanctuary of Asklepius consisted of a spring surrounded by a holy wood and by a clinic that is the so called Adyton; recovery came after a dream that was probably provoked artificially.
However it was not only produced by suggestion, but also by surgical operations and medicines. Pilgrims and patients opened their spirit to hope by admiring and reading the votive offerings and the thanking inscriptions of the people benefitted by the God were hanging on the walls of the temple as symbols of their recognition.

Hendrike Schoof

In order to lift the blocks of stone and other heavy materials, both the Greeks and the Romans used derrick cranes that according to Vitruvius could lift a six ton weight. The difference between that derrick crane and a modern one simply consists of the fact that ours are driven by an engine, while the ancient ones were moved by men. As a matter of fact, slaves made the wheel of the winch turn by using the muscles of their legs; thanks to a system of pulleys, it pulled the rope that held the stone thus lifting it up.

TEMPLE OF OLYMPIAN ZEUS

The great size and the massive walls represented the Agrigentans' pride, who according to the Greek habit, built a monument of victory in gratitude for their victory at Himera (480 - 479 B.C.) over the Carthaginians.

This building was one of the grandest of antiquity. It was made in order to thank Zeus, the most important divinity of the Agrigento Pantheon. It is basically Doric in style. It was the only pseudoperipteron temple, that is, around it there was not the normal colonnade of free-standing columns, but a series of half-columns: seven along the short sides and fourteen along the wall on the back of which they shaped into squared pilasters. It was a heptastyle temple as the number of the front columns was seven: it is the only temple of the town with an odd number of columns along its front.

The great rectangular platform standing on five steps faced

East and was 113.20 m. long, 56 m. wide; it covered a double squared area of 6,407 mq., that is almost as big as a stadium that can contain 42 thousand spectators.

The cella was unroofed as it was a hypetral building. The engaged columns that reached according to Pr. Anselmo Prado a height of 16.88 m. were extrimily thick: the diameter of the base was 4.22 m., that is they are as wide as a room in a house of to-day. Diodorus Siculus pointed out that the 10 flutes of the half-columns were so wide that the body of a man could be contained in each of them: indeed, they were wide from 50 to 63 cm.

The wide intercolumnations were covered with Telamones which are also called Atlantes. They used to stand on plinths half of the height of the walls and supported together with the half-columns the weight of a heavy trabeation with their raised arms.

However, several questions about this temple have not been answered, yet. It is not known where the Telamones, giant male characters that were 7.61 m. tall, actually stood. One of them lying on the ground among the ruins of the temple looks like a God who is having an everlasting sleep. Atlas, a giant son of Jupiter and Asia, was condemned to support the world on his shoulders because he had helped the Titans.

Entrances consisted of two gates on the outer intercolumnations of the east side. A sculptured block that can be seen to the South-East of the east front is thought to be an element of the upper part of the doorway. Two more gates may have been placed on the west side.

To the South, among the ruins a block shaped like the talon of a leg was found 30 m. away from a majestic capital. This sug-

Temple of Olympian Jupiter: reconstruction (picture of the Museo Civico).

Winckelman said that the eight columns of the façade of St. Peter Church in Rome, which is the biggest church of the world, have a diameter which is smaller than those of the Agrigento temple. Wolfang Goethe who came to Agrigento in April 1787 says that 22 people standing side by side can make a circle as wide as the circumference of such a column.

In order to check if the statement made by Diodorus Sicolous was right, the Baron of Riedesel stood in the flute of a column and said excitedly that the temple had to be bigger and nicer than St. Peter Curch in Rome.

A GREEK TEMPLE: isometric cut-away

gests that there were Cariathids, giant female characters that supported the trabeation instead of columns. However, it is not known where such giant statues used to be placed. The relief in which the heroes were portrayed in a manner appropriate to their role, represented the traditional subject of the battle between the Gods and the Giants on the east side and some episodes of the capture of Troy on the west side. A 78 cm. long lion tail sculptured in relief into a block of sandstone and that can be seen to the North-East of the temple, may represent Dyonisius turning into a lion in order to kill the giant Euritius. According to Diodorus the characters had a realistic size. Moreover he says that the temple was unfinished and unroofed. Actually, it was technically very difficult to roof this temple.

Even if there are so many ruins, they look few compared to the size of the building. Many blocks were carried away for building the wharf of Porto Empedocle at the time of Charles III of Bourbon. Historian Tommaso Fazello who can be considered

54

In the quarry the stone was cut in blocks by means of bits that the workers hit with wooden mallets. The blocks were detached from the rock underneath by inserting wooden wedges over which they poured water in order to expand them. For cutting the stone, the workers dug around each block a cutting that was only 50-60 cutting cm. wide. In order to cut the drums of the columns they made a cutting as deep as the diameter of the column they wanted to obtain. At the end the base of the drum was detached with the wooden wedges.

Stone transport by a kind of sledge.
After being modelled, the blocks were carried to the site by sledging them over ramps made of stone and wooden sleepers (similar to the railroad ones). Before the sledge they used to pour water in order to let it slide better.

The hecatomb or mass sacrifice of one hundred bulls

The most significant and customary act of Greek worship was sacrifice (every gift offered to the gods to demonstrate submission, reverence and thanks and to receive grace).

Exceptionally great, they were able to offer many victims in sacrifice, the mass sacrifice of a hundred oxen was called "hecatomb" a word still used to indicate "great slaughter-great number of victims". The picture shows the cerimony of a hecatomb celibrated in public. The victims, chosen among the healthiest and those without defects, were brought to the alter. Before offering the sacrifice, a cup of wine was poured over the victims head, over which barley flour and salt were then sprinkled, some hairs were then ripped from the forehead and thrown into the fire. Once the beasts were killed, the blood was collected in a vase and sprayed onto the alter and asperged on the people present. The meat was divided into portions: the god's portion was burned, a portion was given to the priests and the third portion was divided between the offerer and his friends.

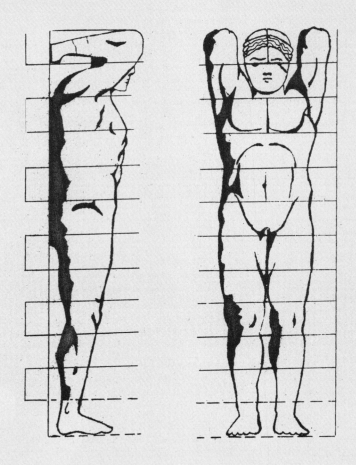

An engaged column of the temple of Olympian Jupiter that turns into a pilaster on the inside.

drawing by Hendrike Schoof

the discoverer of this grand temple, said that the last standing remanins fell on December the 9th 1401.

One of the questions that raises the visitors' interest concerns both the transportation and the building methodes. From a technical point of view everything needed to build a temple, except for the lime that was not used yet, was prepared on the site.

The architect gave precise measurements and plans thus construction mainly consisted of dry-assembling the different elements that after were coated with stucco and decorated. The blocks were shaped at the quarry.

The u-shaped grooves that can still be seen in several blocks were used for containing the ropes of the winches needed for lifting up the blocks.

However, because of the great height of 32.98 m. of the temple, we cannot reject the hypothesis that the Agrigentans used the inclined plane technique like the Egyptians. The first blocks were lifted up with winches. Then each block was carried to its right position over rollers and with tongs that left on the blocks marks that can still be seen. Then, the holes for the lead joints of the drums were cut with bits.

In front of the eastern end of the temple and 47 m. away from it you can see the remains of a big altar where even one hundred oxen could be sacrificed at once. According to tradition the Syracusans used to celebrate the expulsion of the tyrant Thrasibulos by sacrifying 450 bulls to Zeus the Liberator. The building where this grand sacrificial ceremony used to take place consists of a rectangular base that is 56 m. by 12 m. and it could be used by almost 2,000 faithful.

ARCAIC ALTARS ARRANGED IN A PAIR AND THE THESMOFORIA RITE

A pair of arcaic altars of the Vht century B.C. are very interesting both from a religious and from an artistic point of view. The rounded one is hollow in the middle for receiving the faithful's offering. On the other hand the squared flat one was used for sacrificing animals as it is still shown by red traces of fire.

During three days those women who participated to the Tesmophoriae feasts were compelled to abstinence and those men who entered the temple were condemned to die. Another rule to respect was that one of seating over different kinds of aphrodisiac plants.

61

Usually in the Greek world, rounded buildings were used for sacrificial worships. It seems that this rounded altar was used for such purpose because some votive offerings were found inside its hollow.

The Thesmoforia ceremonies in honour of Demeter the supreme Goddess of fertility and the ruler and patroness of marriage were reserved to those women who were married (single women, prostitutes and men could not take part in them).

On the occasion of these yearly feast, during one of which Phalaris proclaimed himself tyrant of Agrigento, some matrons used to put inside the hollow of the rounded altar bread shaped like either phalluses or snakes and female small pigs that were left there to die of starvation.

Tony Pecoraro

VALLONE DELLA COLIMBETRA

In Autumn their remains were collected and mixed with seeds in order to guarantee fertility. According to Kirk the meaning of this ceremony was connected to the magic of fertility. In the Summer, symbols of the generating power of nature and of life that starts again, such as phalluses and snakes, were used in agricultural season. In Autumn, the seeds mixed with the offerings having gained the power of fecundity underground, were supposed to guarantee a rich crop for the next agricultural season. The last day was dedicated to celebrate purification before parturition by performing sacred dances, sacrifices, ritual obscenities and by manipulating objects that represented female sexual organs. Obviously, obscenity was a widespread ritual practice particularly useful for keeping evil spirits away and for increasing fertility.

TEMPLE OF CASTOR AND POLLUX

The temple of Castor and Pollux (Greek Gods corresponding to the Roman Dioscuri) is the symbol of artistic Agrigento. The twins Castor and Pollux were the children of Leda, the beautiful queen of Sparta, and Jupiter who had turned himself into a swan. The first one, a good horse-tamer, was mortal, while Pollux, a boxing champion was immortal.

They protected both the athletes and the hosts and guided the sailors. They took part in the expedition of the Argonauts for capturing the Golden Fleece. They set their sister Helen free when she was imprisoned in the fortress of Afidna at the age of ten. Moreover they chased the pirates away from the Egean archipelago. God Poseidon named Castor and Pollux rescuer of ships in danger and gave them the power of sending favourable winds. As soon as a sacrifice of a white lamb was made on the prow of any ship (black lambs were sacrificed to storm) they arrived blowing in the sky.

After Castor was killed by Ida because he had kidnapped his girlfriend, Pollux who was immortal asked Jupiter either to let him share his brother's destiny or to let his brother live. Jupiter fulfilled his request by letting them live one day each that is everytime Castor came back to life Pollux died and the other way round. Moreover, he put the constellation of Gemini in the sky where when a star rises the other sets.

The naturalistic meaning of this myth can be easily caught. They represented the phenomena of light, particularly light fighting against the enemies, probably the twilight of both morning and evening, that is they personified both morning and evening Venus.

However, beside any naturalistic interpretation, the twins are an example of virtues to the young: an invitation to love each other like brothers do, to share God's gifts, to love each other against the enemies of pubblic wealth and to be kind to everybody: these are the virtues represented by Castor and Pollux. The twins were so venerated that women used to swear before Castor and men before Herakles; both of them before Pollux.

Both Greek and Roman traditions are rich of wonderful episodes concerning these two brothers.

Usually they were portrayed as two smart young boys wearing a light cloak while bridling white wild horses. Moreover, they had an egg-shell shaped hat with a shining star on the top.

Pausania said that they layed in wait for credulous spirits and surprised them.

This temple faces East. The high base on the top of three steps was 34.12 m. by 15.86 m. and covered the area of an almost double square of 541.143 sq.m.

Today, only four out of 34 original columns stand among its remains. It had 6 columns on the front and 13 (the corner ones

included) on each side. They consist of three sandstone drums with 20 sharp edged flutes and are 4.27 m. and 1.10 m. thick.

This temple had a varying and rich decoration. At the corner of the temple there is a very lovely rose, while along the sides of the roof one can see an example of a lion that had a red tongue. The role of the lion in this temple as well as in the temples of Demeter and of Herakles, was to frighten evil spirits and keep them magically away. Their decorative beauty belies the aim they were made for: first of all they were aggressive guardians. Usually, masks of lion had blue manes, yellow muzzles and red tongues that were used for drainage. Heads of lions were alternated with either red or dark blue antefissae representing palmettes, symbols of triumph. A brilliant colourful decoration on top of the stucco was the final touch.

In 1836 the building was cleared of all the blocks and remains that had been covering it for a long time.

Villareale and Cavallari were the archeologists who cleared the base on behalf of the Duke of Serradifalco. They excavated several columns and reconstructed three of them on top of three steps. One more column and the trabeation decorated with a carved echinus was added in 1856. The Duke of Serradifalco who was named keeper of the archeological exavations, stated rightly that this temple was built during the Greek time (480-460 B.C.) and restored by the Romans (Ist century B.C.).

TEMPLE OF VULCAN

Today only two columns and a badly preserved base constitute the remains of the temple of Vulcan.

This temple was almost certainly dedicated to Vulcan since according to Solinus that temple stood near a lake that had made both ancient and modern writers tell stories about oil floating on the water. Among them there was Riesedal who was chased by Mr. Ficani who emptied a leather bag of oil onto the lake before showing it to him.

This temple built in around 430 B.C. faces East. It is 37.89 m. by 19.26 m. and it was surrounded by 34 columns (6 by 13), six of which used to stand on the fronts and 13 on each side. Columns consist of 5 sandstone drums and are 6.30 m. high. You have the chance to see to the South-West of this temple two unfluted drums.

Hephaistos that corresponds to the Roman Vulcan was the God of industry and work. He was ugly and married Venus who betrayed him several times. He had his workshop under Mount Etna where he used to make thunderbolts for Zeus helped by the Cyclops.

CHURCH OF SANTA MARIA DEI GRECI

The church with three naves of Santa Maria dei Greci in the street of the same name, stands over the ruins of the temple of Athena.

To the West there are the remains of the temple that is 34.50 m. by 15 m. It was surrounded by 34 columns (6 by 13), six of which were on the fronts and thirteen on the sides. The foundation of the church is dated back to the XIIth century. Its timber roof is similar to the roof of the Cathedral of Agrigento. Inside the church there is a marble sarcophagus dated 1570 that contains the bones of two Palermo nobles. The doorway is in arabic and norman style.

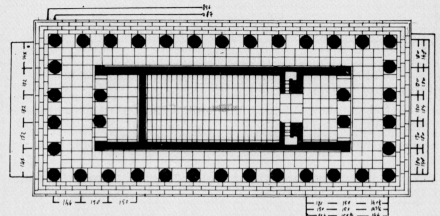

Temple of hera (Juno) Plan (Mertens' hypothesis)

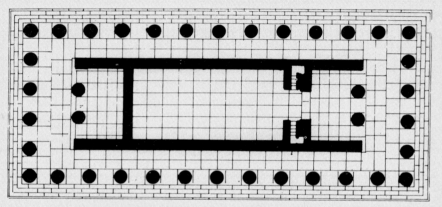

Temple of concord

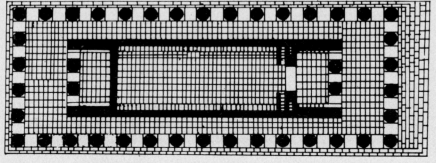

Plan (Rieman's hypothesis) Temple of Herakles (Hercules)

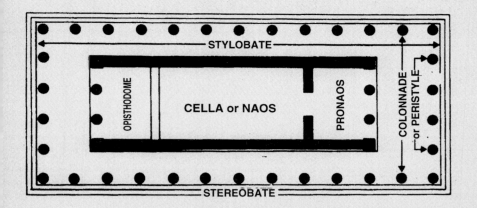

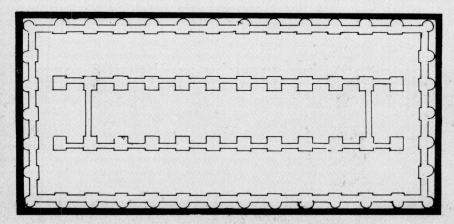

The Plan of Olympian Zeus   Plan (Dinsmoor's hypothesis)

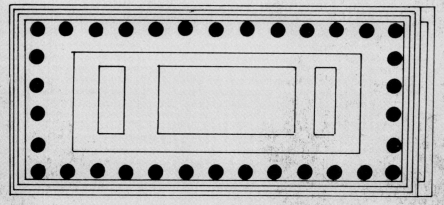

Temple of Castor and Pollux   Plan (De Wale's hypothesis)

giuseppe di giovanni

SELINUNTE

IL PARCO ARCHEOLOGICO

MUSEO
Regionale Archeologico

R. COKERELL, 1830

NATIONAL ARCHEOLOGICAL MUSEM

Free entrance; it is open every day.
From Monday to Saturday: from 9.00 a.m. to 5.00 p.m.
Sundays and holidays: from 9.00 a.m. to 12.30 a.m.

1 – PANCRAZI
2 – PACE
3 – GABRICI
4 – KOLDEWEY
5 – SERRA DI FALCO
6 – CAVALLARI
7 – SCHUBRING
8 – COLUMBA
9 – SALINAS
10 – VILLAREALE
11 – POLITI
12 – ORSI
13 – ZANOTTI BIANCO
14 – EMANUELE RIZZO
15 – NAVARRA
16 – PARETI
17 – LIBERTINI
18 – SINATRA
19 – PICONE
20 – FAZELLO
21 – MARCONI

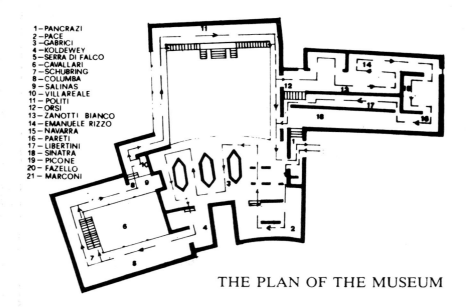

THE PLAN OF THE MUSEUM

Room n. 1 - « Giuseppe Pancrazi » Ancient sources and general topography.

The pannels on the front walls quote Pindar, Empedocles, Virgil and Quasimodo and what they have written about Akrakas, a town that was founded in 581 B.C. by Rhodian and Cretan colonists. To the left, an archeological plan of the town shows that the urban area covered 456 hectares and was surrounded by defensive walls that were 13 km. long. According to Politi and to Pardi the population consisted of 600,000 while from Laertio's standpoint there lived 800,000 people. After Ehrenberg's studies it can be stated that in Akragas there lived approximately 40,000 citizens with full rights, that is 150,000 if we consider their families, too; moreover there were between 10 and 15 thousand foreigners living in the town that is almost 40,000 people with their families included and 110,000 slaves many of which worked in the fields and slept outside the town. On the whole, as Picone states, there lived 300,000 people. On the left wall you can see some enlarged reproductions of old prints representing Agrigento that were taken from a book written in 1750 by Theatine Giuseppe Pancrazi who gives his name to this room.

Room n. 2 - « Biagio Pace ». Pre-greek time and colonization (cases no. 1-10).

The collection displayed in ten cases of this room is exhibited in a topographical order. All the objects coming from the same archeological site are shown in the ten cases of this room next to which you can see large topographic plans on which the areas where they were found are marked.

The first case holds objects from the eneolothic station of Serrafirlicchio (Middle Eneolithic 2600-2400 B.C.) which has the same name of the site in the North of Agrigento where it was found.

On the Serrafirlicchio pottery a dull black colour covers a chamois reddish surface which is decorated with stripes, wolf's teeth and hour-glasses..

In the second case you can see the archeological findings from the prehistorical necropolis of Monserrato near Agrigento. The typical Castelluccio pottery has a chamois colour and is simply decorated with blackish lines painted on an either reddish or yellowish background. The name of this particular kind of pottery comes from the village and from the rocky necropolis of Castelluccio (near Syracuse) that dates from early Bronze Age (1900-1450 B.C). The study of the clay objects among which there are mainly small dipping cups, bowls and biconical cups shows

that they were used for carrying out worships connected with the element of water and its role in the economy of primitive communities. Probably it consisted of offering a libation and also of offering the same vase that had just been used for the libation of the God.

Interesting items:

73

(2/R/D) a biconical cup with two handles between the pedestal and the basin decorated with geometrical patterns that produce grid bands. Probably the remarkable height of the vase was due to the habit of eating on the floor with the cup that reached the height of one's chest.

In the third case you can see early bronze age pottery (1990-1450 B.C.) that was found in the archeological site of Montaperto that belongs to the Castelluccio culture.

The objects that are worth to see are:

(2/R/S) a large jug with three handles decorated with bands of descending lines. It was a water container: the big handle was used in order to get the water from the spring, while the side ones allowed to hold it on one's head and to carry it;

A jar made of impasto, a prehistoric vase used for the conservation of the ashes of a deseased person. In the home it was used for cooking.

(2/S) A small Mycenean amphora which takes its name from the site of Mycene in Argolis. It is a great example of globular amphora with three handles on the back. This nice little vase was a luxury and it was probably exported as parfum container for the high society.

(1/R/D) a dipping bowl with surmounting handle, that is a prehistorical cup.

In the fourth case there are the archeological findings from the prehistorical site of Cannatello (a village of late Bronze Age 1250 - half of the 8th century B.C.) and from the seaside of Agrigento. These are very rich objects that the Myceneans gave the Sicans in exchange for metal objects such as axes, swords, lances (utensil currency) and magnificent clay vases in exchange for cereals (such as wheat, barley, wine) and beautiful horses. Their use as objects accompanying the dead shows that they were probably used as coins paying for the journey to the Underworld. These findings let us realize that those Myceneans pointed out the Greek colonists the sea route to follow and the fertile lands to conquer.

(2/R/D) A bronze fibula with a simple curve, that is a safety pin. But the fibula is more famous because of a peculiar episode that we do not know if it has actually taken place. According to Herodotus in 568 B.C., the Athenians were terribly defeated. Only one warrior survived and hardily he managed to reach Athens and to give the news. Women maddened by grief surrounded him and as he hesitated before answering they took their fibulas from their peplos and started to prick him.

Since then a decree forbed Athenian women to wear the peplos, thus they substituted it with a tunic with bottons that unlike fibulas were harmless.

Thus the frocks 'a sacque', held by one shoulder only, disappear from Greek fashion to make way for the tunic, fastened with buttons, and so creating the first revolution in women's fashion.

(2/R/C) A bronze axe with a stepping out fin tapered in the middle and a hole for the wooden hafts.

(2/R/D) A sward, a war armament and a symbol of power with three holes for the hafts. It is an old symbol of royalty. According to archeologist Giuseppe Castellana, bronze armaments were made by the Sican artisans out of Aegean-Mycenean ones.

(2/R/C) Four points of lance either war or hunting armaments with a tube for the wooden stick (a cannon like lance) and a hole for the holding nail.

In the fifth case you can see objects dating from late Bronze Age and Iron Age that corresponds to the time of the early Greek immigration to the Agrigento area of S. Angelo

Muxaro. These objects come from the large necropolis of domeshaped tombs of the ancient Sicanian site, that is thought to be the king Kokalos' town of Kamikos. These are fragments of nicely shaped pottery made on the wheel where the row surface was

painted in reddish colour.
Both in the sixth and in the

seventh cases set into the wall, there are the findings dating from the 8th century B.C. that were found in Gela, Licata and Palma di Montechiaro. The exhibited objects are quite interesting because they show the early characteristics of Greek religion which was connected with the Gods of fertility, with the changing of seasons, with births, with the ritual of death and resurrection in the Underworld and with the role that apotropaic objects (against evil eye) had during worship.

(2/R/R - Ag 9645) A clay head of bull: this character reminds us of the famous legend of the bronze bull of Phalaris, the cruel tyrant of Agrigento (from 570 till 554 B.C.) who made it red-hot after having locked up his enemies inside it.

Their cries of pain sounded outside like natural roars of a real bull.

That legend comes from the propitiatory sacrifice of rain to God Helios made by the Rhodian colony of Agrigento that had as symbol a bronze bull (Pindar - Pitica no, 1 - 185): the cries similar to the roars of a bull produced storms.

(1/R/C) A small clay altar with two sphynx facing one another. Sphynx that symbolized strength and intelligence with its body of lion, its breast of woman and its wings of eagle, is often represented in Greek iconography. It was not only the highest example of art of that time but it was also an apotropaic symbol. It is one of those magic symbols that were used for protecting a person, a house or even a town against evil eye. It seems that sphynx symbolized the plague that often affected the Theban territory. The ancient were superstitious and if a cat crossed the path, before going on their way, they either threw three stones to the other side of the path or they waited for somebody to go first.

Demetra sitting on the throne.

Here the Goddess Demetra is portrayed as Her Majesty the Goddess.

The beautiful goddess is sitting on a high-backed throne, to ensure a comfortable position there is also a foot-stool. The term 'throne', a symbol of royal power for the Greeks, meant the seat of the Lord, the Dominator,

the invention of which can be traced back to the precautions taken by the King, who was afraid of being knifed from behind by any possible aspirants to the throne.

(2/R/D) A clay oscillum on which you can see represented a four arm swastika. It is a rounded disk that used to be hung on the eaves of houses against the evil eye. It consists of a cross with four arms that have all the same length which make a right angle by bending towards the left. It is an arhaic

comes from Palma di Montechiaro. A scene painted on it represents the Triquetra (Triskeles with three legs), that is the

symbol of the triangular shape of Sicily from which the ancient name of the island comes from.

It is a swastika with three arms and with three legs running one after the other, symbol of the sun represented in triple shape as God of Spring, of Summer and of Winter.

symbol of the sun rotation and of the sun as God of Spring, Summer, Autumn, a season which is not represented by the Triquetra on the dinos, and of Winter.

Case no, 7

(2/R/D) A dinos made in Gela (inv. 4328). It was a pot used for libations, that is a main object for worshipping the dead. It dates back to about the end of the 7th century B.C. and

(1/R/C) Weights of loom: pierced objects which have the shape of truncated pyramids. They were religious objects connected with the worship of the Goddess Mother of fertility. The ancients propitiated rain by turning those weights around after having hung them on a string. This was how they imitated the sound of the wind

THE THOPHET
THE CRUEL SACRIFICE OF CHILDREN
BESTOWED BY CARTHAGINIANS
TO GODS BAAL AND TANIT

This religious ceremony is admirably narrated by Diodorus Siculus in one of his best kown passages: « there was made by the Carthaginians a bronze statue of Cronus who angled his open hands downward so that the children would roll from them and hurl down into a fire pit. Their relatives were present, but they were forbidden to cry in order to prevent them from reducing with their sorrow the value of the sacrifice which would lead to the divinization of the sacrificed children ». The custom of sacrificing children from the best families is related to the rite of offering the early fruits to the divinities.
Diodorus Siculus reports that in 310 B.C., the citizens wanted to redeem themselves from the error of having substituted the children from the best families for acquired children, and ordered the sacrifice of 200 children.

while they produced the roars of thunder by beating a well stretched ox leather; two lighted torches imitated the flashes of lightening.

After this ceremony that propitiated rain, the weights were hung on a tree. Then, they waited for the rain. In a bridal procession some girls preceded the bride by holding wool wound on a distaff, the weights of loom, a spindal with threads of wool and a pot of barely; the whole thing symbolized the duties of the wife as householder.

In the cases no, 8-9-10 you can see the late Corinthian objects and the Rhodian plates that came from the necropolis of Maddalusa (in San Leone). In the case no, 10 there are fragments of Corinthian pottery decorated with web-footed birds, lions, a bull and a panther, that remind you of the decorations of oriental dapestry.

Room no, 3 - « Ettore Gabrici » (cases no, 11-41). The vase collections.

A few steps lead to the most important room which is said to be the « great room of the figurative art masterpieces ». Indeed all the 150 vases can be defined as such; they are exhibited and illuminated in such a wonderful way that all details can be examined. There is a wide choice of vases to describe. However, I will give a short description of them from the historical and mythological point of view. From my standpoint they are worthy seeing even for the rushed visitors who should not only admire them but should also understand the meaning of the scenes depicted on them. Vases do not represent only a highly developed craftmanship, but also a civilization that no one else has ever managed to revive. The Greeks used

Above: the vase collection room.

Potters and vase decorators at work

The ceramists were at the same time producers and sellers of their goods. The picture represents the potter and painter working together in the same workshop.

On the stove one can see holes to regulate the heat (the valves are visible on the shelves hanging on the wall). The clay was extracted from Ceramico, on the outskirts of Athens, from which we get the name "ceramic".

drawings to depict the meaning of their myths and of their way of living: they narrated by drawing.

But it has to be pointed out that the authors of Agrigento vases are unfortunately anonymous. As a consequence of that on the didactic plates shown next to the vases of which we do not know the name neither of the painter nor of the potter, you can read either « Berlin Painter » or « Edimbourgh Painter » according to the place where you can see the masterpiece made in the same style. But when you read for instance « Pan Painter », that means that the potter's name was Pan.

It is worthy saying something about the technique which has given such great charm to the clay art of the 6th and 5th century B.C.. Recently, some German and British chemists and archeologists have found out that the famous black paint is not an actual paint. The thin film was obtained with a solution of pure clay which was previously ground and made very fine, from which they made water to evaporate until they obtained a kind of dark brown liquid jelly. Such a colloidal solution was spread with a brush over the smooth surface of the clay vase before baking it. Then the oven was highly overheated till the temperature reached 800, 945 and 875 decrees C.. Historian Alessio Narbone says that the clay of an attic vase which was analysed by chemist Antonio Furitano, consisted of 40% silica, 16% alluminium, 14% carbonic substances. This is a chemical compound which gave the vase lightness and durability against melting in the oven and against humidity.

After this short introduction, it is time to enjoy the visit to this room.

(1/R/S) Crater with small column-shaped handles on which you can see depicted a scene representing lions attacking a bull.

Greek wines especially the Sicilian ones were full-bodied and had a very high alcoholic content. That is why in order to drink a lot of wine it was worthy diluting it. The container used for mixing wine with water was the crater. The shape and the wide belly of this vase are due to the fact that it held another vase full of snow, ice, fresh or hot water according to the desired temperature of the wine. The latter vase floated in the wine. One of the most commonly used mixtures consisted of one third wine mixed with two thirds water. They used to mix the wine with honey in or-

Zenith while the constellation of Taurus disappears beyond the horizon.

As Delatte says, Spring is not a season like the others, but a break in time that indicates both the renewal of the products of the ground and the exhaustion of human reserves. Spring is the season when human activities start: harvests, wars, sailing.

(1/R/D) A crater with small column-shaped handles with a Corinthian influenced animal decoration.

On this black-figure crater, a vase used for mixing water with wine, that dates from about 550 B.C., the painter has depicted Ephaistos, the patron of smiths, going back to Mount Olympus. As his mother Hera, that is Juno for the Romans, thought that he was too ugly,

der to give it the flavour of different flowers thus obtaining the « mulsum »; sometimes they even put it on the loft inside small barrels and there they let it absorbe the smoke thus calling it « fumosum ».

On the black-figure crater dating from 550 B.C. on which you can see depicted lions attacking a bull, the painter symbolizes the feast of Spring. The lions attacking the bulls is indeed a subject represented even in the Dario's Palace in Persepolis that according to W. Hartner has to be considered from an astronomical point of view. It represents the feast of Spring: the last week of March the constellation of Leo is at the

she threw him from Mount Olympus down to the Earth. Since then he has kept on meditating to take a revenge for that act. He then gave his mother a golden throne, a great example of his skill. His mother sat on it but she was not able to get up any more. She was set free thanks to Dionysius, the God of wine, who promised him Aphrodite in marriage. Hence, with his mind under the influence of wine, but happy, he went back to Olympus and Hera a was set free from the throne. In such a way the grim and ugly Hephaistos managed to marry Aphrodite the embodiment of beauty.

It is evident that the Greeks amused themselves about this contrast that on the other hand points out that some-times success at work can be rewarded with beauty. The scene depicted on the vase shows Hephaistos armed with a double-edged axe while he is riding the ithyphallic mule. The procession is led by a very elegant and lovely Maenad dressed with the skin of a wild animal who is holding a gift probably a hare. Under the influence of an orgiastic passion she is going to cut that animal into pieces and to eat it in order to nourish her body but also for assimilating its vital power according to omophagic ceremonies. This sacrifice symbolized how Winter damages all products of the ground: it is a ceremony of death and resurrection.

An inebriated and dancing Satyr is showing his virtues openly. Behind him one can see a procession of characters who are holding a kantharos (this is the name of a cup with high handles so that your did not wet your hands). Dance points out the power of nature to grant the grouth of children, sheep, grains and trees. Satyrs, half-goats, who loved wine and all kind of pleasures followed Dionysius in procession while holding the Phallos (male sex), that is the symbol of the generating power of nature. It is a religious scene as the drunkness of Dionysius and of the characters following him in procession was considered as divine frenzy. The ceremonial nudity and the exhibition of sexes which have a fecunding power are also used against evil eye and for keeping all misfortunes away. This vase that we do not where it was found, is cm. 37.7 high and has a cm. 31.7 long diameter.

Case no, 18

(2/R/D) A lekythos with a scene representing Herakles' victory against the Chercops, the thieves.

The Chercops were a kind of clever and malicious elves who had taken the precaution of disarming him while he was asleep. Herakles carried them away upside down with their

84

Shapes of greek vases

Kantharos

Skyphos

Kylix

Stamnos

Lekythos

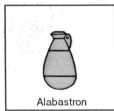

Alabastron

Amphoreus

Pelike

Deinos

Hydria

Aryballos

Krater

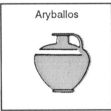

Voluten
krater

shaped crater that dates from about the 5th century B.C., the Pezzino Painter has depicted on a shining black background a scene of death. This scene shows the body of the hero Patroclus lying on the catafalque while his soul is leaving his body for the Hades which has the same name of its King. All characters are Spartan citizens as it is shown by their long hair. This was a symbol of those citizens who enjoyed full rights. Later the same habit was followed by the Vandals who cut the Roman's hair to represent their submission.

On the back side you can see a scene representing the solemn funerals that were made in honour of Patroclus.

Case no, 25

(2/R/C) A crater with small column-shaped handles on which you can see depicted a

fest tied to a stick and carried them as if they were animals.

The Chercops were mischivious and showed up under shape of deceptive dreams. They could be driven out by invoking Herakles who was the only one who had the power over nightmares.

Case no, 19

(2/R/C) A crater on which you can see depicted a scene of death by Pezzino Painter.

On this red figure globet-

scene representing a leavetaking.
On this red figure crater the Leningrad Painter has represented on the left a white-haired old man who is wearing a cloak and is leaning on a cane. He seems to be giving advice to an ephebus, that is an adolescent who had reached the age of 18 and had been in the army for 24 months. This scene emanates feeling: by giving advice, the father hides the fact that he is sorry for their separation and that he is worried because it could become final. On the left another ephebus is holding a sword while talking to a girl who is holding a helmet and a lance.

(2/R/D) A crater showing a scene representing Dionysius by the Pan Painter.
On this red figure goblet-shaped crater dating from about 460 B.C., the Pan Painter has represented Dionysius, the God of wine, of drama, of fertility and of joy, holding in his left hand a twig of ivy, a dionysiac plant, and a spotted skin on his arm that was an ornament which propitiated rain fall. The vase was found in a necropolis of Agrigento and is 42 cm. high and has a 37.3 cm. diameter.

Case n. 26

(1/R/C) A crater with a scene representing Herakles and Nes-

sus by the Agrigento Painter.
A red figure goblet-shaped crater with a scene representing Herakles and Nessus that dates from about 475-450 B.C. on which the Agrigento Painter has depicted the centaur Nessus who is attempting to kidnap Deianira, Herakles' second wife. Along the way Nessun tried to chase her violenty and this provoked the hero who killed the centaur, a half man and half horse being. While he was dying he took revenge and adviced

Red figure attic crater representing a sacrifice to Apollo (the Kleophon painter, 430 B.C.)

Deianira to collect his blood. « If one day Herakles will leave you » he said « then you will have to dip his clothes into my blood in order to regain his love ». Sometime later, Herakles took as a prisoner a beautiful princess. Jealous Deianira dipped a nice tunic she had woven for her husband into Nessus blood. But the blood had been poisoned by Herakles' arrow and as soon as he wore it he was attacked by the acute pains. That was Nessus' revenge: Herakles had to dye.

This vase that was found in the rock of Monserrato in 1877 is 40.2 cm. high and has a 40 cm. diameter.

(2/R/C) A crater with a dionysiac scene by the Louvre Painter.

On this red figure crater with small column-shaped handles that dates from about 440 B.C., the Louvre Centauromachia Painter has depicted two ephebus engaged in a sports competition in honour of Dionyisius.

For the Greeks a sports compition was a religious ceremony. The participants were the all-round athletes who had the power of speed, the attribute of the Gods par excellence. The left side of the scene is occupied by a discobolus. One can admire the athletic perfection of his body and the sense of movement that the artist was able to depict. The other figure represents a young athlete while he is throwing the javelin. The exercises of the two young boys are marked by the flute player.

In Greece women were stricthy excluded from the gymnasiunm, a place reserved for physical exercise. Any women found entering the gymnasium were punishable with the death penalty. Although history tells us (as referred by Sabatino Moscati) of a mother, who in order to be with her son whilst taking part in a competition, did not hesitate to disguise herself as a trainer. She entered the field as such and when her son succeeded victorious ran to meet and embrace him, unfortunately, she was betrayed by her dress, which lifted itself up whilst she ran and thus her sex was revealed.

The judges of the competition were touched by her actions and she was pardoned - from that moment on instruction were given to the trainers to enter the stadium nude, as did all the other athletes.

A curious point concerns

PEOPLE PLAYING THE KOTTABOS GAME

Symposia were arranged by a well-off person and the guests participated to them gladly. This game consisted of flicking a small amount of wine at a small balanced dish thus making it fall below on the hard plate fixed to half height of a stand; the winner had the preemptive right of taking the beautiful flute-girl who had beeb hired for the party. She had to be able to play, to dance and to abandon herself to venal love.

the caloric diet; the athletes were nourished with three kilogrammes of meat each, in comparison to the three thousand calories consumed daily by rich Greek and Roman men.

Case no, 27

(1/R/C) A globet-shaped crater with a scene representing a sacrifice to Apollo made by the

Kleophon Painter.

This globet-shaped crater probably painted by the Kleophon Painter (about 430 B.C.) and found in the necropolis of Poggio Giache, represents a scene of sacrifice to Apollo as it is shown by the twigs of laurel. Starting from the right, the scene represents 5 men and an animal. It shows a flute player whose music marks the holy ce-

On the white crater of 430 B.C., the Phiale Painter has depicted a scene concerning Perseus. He is wearing a sleeveless white chiton, a hat, the perasos and winged shoes while holding with his right hand two lances that he is going to use for setting Anromache free. She is tied to three poles. She is the daughter of Cepheus and Cassiopea, the rulers of Ethiopia. She is as strong as a man: indeed her name is « Andromache » that is the Greek word for « man »,

remony. The second character is a goat that is standing by the rounded altar: it is held by an assistant and it is going to be sacrificed. This is the most importat moment before the main part of the ceremony that consisted of killing the victim while holding its head backwards in such a way that the blood spilling out abundantly flowed over the altar. Between two columns that represent the temple, Apollo is sitting confortably on his throne while holding a twig of laurel that is one of his symbols. Apollo was the God of light and truth, the God of spring rebirth who guarantees the good order of seasons. He was venerated in Agrigento and people came from everywhere in order to ask for his advice and help.

(2/R/C) The crater with a scene representing Andromache's

« male ». Between the two characters you can read praise for Eualon, Aeschylus' son. The myth of Perseus symbolizes the victorious fight of the sun against the power of darkness and especially against storm clouds. The crater which was found in 1940 in the necropolis of Caulineddi is 44 cm. high and has a 45 cm. diameter.

(1/R/C) The crater with a scene showing the kottabos game made by the Dinos Painter.

On the red figure crater dating from 420 B.C., the dinos Painter has depicted a scene of symposium (drinking with each other) that used to take place after dinner, while they had the dessert which consisted of nuts, dry figs, chick-peas and roast broad beans. It consisted of drinking with others' good company, while a symposiarch fixed the strength of the wine. Music, dance and talking were the pleasures that men enjoyed

during the after dinner symposium. The guests participated in the kottabos game for obtaining the service of the beautiful hetaer who had been hired for the banquet. They are lying on beds (klinai) below which you can see tables. They hold a cup from which they drink wine while listening to the music played by the Hetaera.

In order to protect themselves against fever and sickness caused by the wine, they are wearing wreaths of blossoms.

Hetaeras were women who were allowed legally to have adulterous sex. Their particular job was that of offering their venal love. They were much requested. Their entertainment after banquet or even during its duration, was considered as an essential need, and important people competed for the services of the most famous hetaeras.

The kottabos game was the most successful Greek game and was performed mainly during banquets: firstly they emptied their cup of wine almost completely, then they threw the last drops of wine onto a plate which was placed in the middle of the room; if they managed to hit the target they gained the woman's services.

(1/R/C) The crater with the scene of the kottabos game made by Pantoxena Painter.

The main character of this scene depicted by the Pantoxena Painter by using the red figure technique in the last quarter of the 5th century B.C., is the banqueter who is playing the Etruscan kottabos game. It

scene representing the corona-tion of Hermes made by the Hearst Painter.

On this protoapulian goblet-shaped crater that dates from

consists of a stick with a small rounded plate on top; the small rounded plate was made to fall underneath onto the hard disc that was fixed at half the height of the stick. This was done by throwing from a certain distance wine from a cup that was held by the edge with one's thumb and index finger. The winner gained the right of preemption over the woman who had been hired for the banquet.

The most widespread kotta-bos game was the sicilian one which could be performed in different ways: by throwing the wine left in one's cup after the libation into the cup of the he-taera to whom they proposed their love, or by trying to hit and to sink by the same means some cups that were floating in a bowl. This crater is 33.9 cm. high and has a 38 cm. diameter.

Case no, 34

(1/R/C) The crater with the

about half of the 5th century B.C., the Hearst Painter has de-picted the coronation of Her-mes, the clever and nice Apollo's brother. The scene shows also a winged nike (the Goddess of Victory). The wings of Victory are wide and open; she is wearing a Doric peplus (a long sleeveless garment that rea-ched one's feet). You can also see a boy: his hair is short. When they became ephebus (that is when they went to the army), young boys cut their hair and offered it to Apollo.

The main scene shows a bear-ded head of Hermes, the God

of roads. He has no arms but an excited male sex (the phallos), the symbol of the generating power of nature that has an apotropaic magic power against evil eye. The pillar is decorated with a caduceus, that is a magic cane around which there used to be two snakes. Hermes used it in order to stop wind and clear the sky. All those who were going to leave the town and the God's protection, that is sheperdes, messengers, traders and even thieves and brigands asked for help to this stone column that usually stood at the border of the town where the closest road started. Country offerings were made and oil was spread. Thus Hermes accompanied them with the help of his wisdom and showed the wayfarer the right way.

One morning of the year 415 B.C. in Athens, just before the departure for Sicily of the Athenian expedition that had been prepared in great detail and that had been approved by all citizens, the hermas of God Hermes were found mutilated. This was considerred bad luck for the enterprise that ended in 413 B.C. with seven thousand survivors used in the Syracusan stone quarries after which they were sold as slaves.

Case no, 36

(27R/S) A plate from Campania decorated by the Dublin Painter

This nice example of a plate from Campania which dates from about 350 B.C., is a fish plate. Fish are finely decorated on it with motives typical from that time: you can see three perfectly simmetrical fish surrounding a little hollow for the garum. This was a sauce in great demand which was made with the viscera and the tails of different kind of fish according to the quality. The use of this product a kind of which can still be found in the town of Trapani, was firstly introduced by the Carthaginians for garnishing meat, fish, lamb and chicken.

A marble torso of warrior

This great example of Attic sculpture dating from 470 B.C. is damaged in several parts. mainly on the nose, on the cheeks, on the chin and on the lips. The simple and natural position of the body and the features of the visage that express a strong physical pain bore with

95

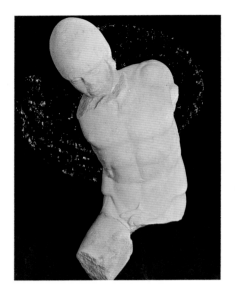

strength, make of this statue attributed to Pythagoras from Reggio, one of the most striking examples of Greek art.

In the small case on the northern wall you can see a complete picture of the figure of the warrior and a few small fragments of the statue.

Room no, 4 - «Kodewey and Puchstein». The architectural sculpture.

This room contains some gutters that were used both in an useful and decorative way in the Greek and Hellenistic architectural decorative art. The role of the lion in the Greek temple was mainly that of frightening the evil and keeping it away magically.

Their decorative beauty is the reason that they were made: first of all they were aggresive guards. On the facing wall there is an exhibition of nine lion heads which have a fiercel feline look with open mouths. Most of them come from the temples of Herakles and of Demeter.

To the left of the Gallery you can see five small simas, that is eaves on which the gutters were engaged. The surface of the si-

mas was decorated with meanders, palmettes and lotuses.

Room no, 5 - «Duca di Serradifalco». Sanctuaries and temples (cases n. 42-65).

The pride of the Museum of Agrigento which distinguishes it from other similar archeological museums, are the stupendous sculptures mainly made of clay which decorated the sanctuaries.

The findings exhibited in this room are many and well made and they are envied by many people as they represent the religious history of that time. It is a way of reviving the supersticious religion of that time. However, in order to understand their inner meaning we will not analyse them from only the technical and aesthetic point of view: we have to try to imagine in those often broken objects their deep human and religious meaning.

The masterpieces of Greek art exhibited in 24 transparent cases hold a significance which is difficult to understand. These works before being decorative objects were holy offerings. Oscillums, Sphinxes, phalluses, Gorgons and Sileni had a religious aim especially against evil eye and against misfortunes. This is why we have tried to describe their meaning, what they were used for and their history.

We point out in the cases the following:

The Mule of Dionysius (inv. S. 65)

You can see this vase which was used for containing liquids known as the Mule of Diony-

sius, which dates from about the 5th century B.C.. This red figure askos, that is an erotic vase for liquids, is interesting because besides the beauty of the animal you can admire a man on his knee: he is under the mule and is holding a cup with his right hand. The ritual nudity of the Satyr and the ithyphallic mule besides having a fertile power, have also a magic aim against evil eye and against misfortune.

A small archaich mask of black man (inv. S. 83).

This archaic mask of a black man that dates from about the 6th C. B.C. is very expressive. It has a realistic look. All its phys-

A pinax, representing a running Gorgon (inv. S. 16).

ical features such as its short hair (the short hair was a characteristic of the slaves, a habit that was later used by the barbarians too, as they cut the Romans' hair as symbol of their submission), its wide and flattened head and its fleshy lips that are precisley represented, give this object a great bright expression.

A faceless clay tube (inv. S. 67)

This object which is still being studied, is a faceless clay tube over which two ears and a female braid are stuck. It is a work that dates from about the 5th C. B.C.. It was used for asking the favour of the cthonian gods, that is the underground gods about wich a study is still under way.

It is a well made mould of a Gorgon, that is a human but monstruous character with pug nose, feline look and open

mouth. She could see from one eye only and she was able to turn all those who looked at her into stone. It is said that it symbolized the vices that lead the young to disgrace. Perseus, who was free from those vices could cut the Medusa's head without being seen. Then he used it for winning against his ennemies. Greek bakers used to depict a head of Gorgon on their ovens in order to stop anybody who wished to open it thus affecting the baking of the bread with a sudden puff of fresh air. The Greeks used to exhibit a Gorgon head over the gates of the town and of their houses in order to keep the evil eye away.

The fact of attacking a house protected in such a way meant to violate the virgin Goddess Athena. This superstition was respected even by the Athenians.

Case no, 49

Oil lamps

Oil lamps which used to contain a combustible liquid that burned and produced fire, had a magic meaning: they were needed for illuminating life and for chasing negative influeces. Oil lamps were widely used by the ancients not only for illuminating the darkness of night, but also during sacrifices, feasts, weddings and in the graves. The exhibited oil lamps were illuminated in front of the statue representing the God.

The head of Demetra with modius, dating back to around the VI century B.C., was so called because on the head was a cup in the shape of a modius (an antique measure for cerials equivalent to a bushel). This was filled with wheat before being brought in votive offering to the temple of Demetra, Goddess of Abundance, as auspice for a good harvest.

The Goddess is adorned with a triple necklace, ornating her breast, decorated with the symbols of abundance and fertility, (Bucrane, the architectonic motive of Doric style represented by the ox-skull, patera, the vase without handles used for libations to the Divinity; silenic heads, water genii, gifted with divinatory powers, used as lucky charms and vases).

A bust representing Kore 3/R (inv. 3450). The feasts of Persephones.

This clay head dating from the 5th C. B.C. points out the beauty of Agrigento kore, a typ-

Agrigento kore
Vth century B.C.

ical local hieratic form created for worshipping Cthonian Gods.

Youthful charm charcterizes this nice figure: a small head, a delicate face and a small nose.

Once Kore who was also called Persephones (the Roman Proserpina), the daughter of Demeter and Jupiter, was kidnapped by Hades (Pluto), the God of Hades while she was picking flowers in a meadow and she was taken to Hell where she became Queen. This myth is very ancient and it has given birth to agricultural cermonies that were propitiatory of fertility.

The Agrigentans performed the Theogamie in honour of Persephones: these were solemn feasts that took place several times during the year; the Anthesphoriae Feasts were celebrated in Spring in order to evoke the rape of Persephones and during which Agrigento virgins performed dances and made bouquets of flowers for the Goddess.

At the beginning of Summer when the wheat is ripe and the vegetation loses its exuberance, it was time to make the Cathagoghes Feasts that celebrated Persephones descending to Hades' kingdom. During these feasts there used to be performed a kind of holy representation of Demeter wandering and looking for her missing daughter. Ceremonies propitiatory of fertility were performed and women made cakes with sesame and honey shaped like female sex (the mylloi) which were taken around in honour of the Goddess in order to propitiate not only the fertility of plants and of human beings, but also in order to cast out natural calamities.

On this occasion women abandoned themselves to lust in honour of Demeter as they thought that by watching those practices she forgot for a while her grief caused by the disappearance of her daughter (this is the meaning of the Goddess' light smile).

The Anagoghes Feasts celebrated Persephones coming back to the Earth with her mother; while during the Anacolipteria Feasts, Agrigento women, like Goddess Persephones opened their veils in front of their husbands who gave them their wedding-gift.

Case no, 51

A head of Athena with a helmet (inv. 1275)

It is a figurine that dates from about 490 B.C. that represents Goddess Athena wearing the helmet that made invisible all those who wore it with a wide neck-guard. The head of the Goddess of arts, of wisdom, of war and sciences who born out from Jupiter's head already

The bronze crater

adult, is represented as a proud and firm woman. Those people who were dying recommended themselves not only to Hermes who guided souls, but also to Athena the Goddess of wisdom, of sciences and art.

chastity and were sacred to Pan; peacocks symbolized pride and were sacred to Hera; doves and swans symbols of simplicity were sacred to Venus; dogs symbols of fidelity were sacred to Artemis; cockrels symbols of control and of waking up in the underworld were sacred to Asklepius. Before dying it was recommended to sacrifice a cockrel to Asklepius that is what Socrates asked for.

Case no, 52

Votive offerings representing animals

In the ancient world some animals had a holy meaning. For instance, turtles symbolized

(1/R) Vase representing the God Bes in relief.

The most interesting object of this part of the collection is the popular ancient Egyptian God Bes. It is a jug shaped like a bearded dwarf considered as the protector of houses and therefore represented in the daily used household furnishing.

*Clay antefissa shaped like a head of silenus and representing the bearded face of the river Acheloo
(5th century B.C.) - (Case 59)*

The 'kernoi', with three to eleven spouts on the border, are characteristic. These lamps, which come from the Sanctuary of Demetra, are in the shape of a disk and are empty in the middle.

A clay head which comes from the Sanctuary of Demetra.

Case no, 55

Fragments of antefix painted with a decoration representing a palmette (inv. S. 24).

It is a nice eave tile that from about the 6th C. B.C.. It is an object as colourful as the land, the sea and the sky of Agrigento which shows a powerful solar nature. Surely the Greeks had a great pictorial taste and they actually loved policromy. The use of colours in architecture had three aims: it made the temple more visible from a certain distance and different from the landscape; it fulfilled the faithful's taste for colours, it preserved both the clay and the plaster.

It can be interesting to know that when women were in labour they used to hold a twig of palm as they thought that tree had the healing virtue of soothing their pains. The palm was a symbol of victory and of happiness, too.

Containers, in the shape of a female head, in which the oils and balms were conserved.

The group of seven containers can be connected to the worship of the magic ritual, for the purification of the body and soul carried out by the ablution of the hands and of the body. If the city was hit by some misadventure solemn ablutions took place in public using holy water, thus activating the purification process. The bath, which can be found in the archeological museum's complex, was used for this.

Case no. 59

A small clay head of Silenus.

Votive clay shots (inv. 6982)

The pannel exhibiting the clay shots, that is clay acorn-shaped missiles that were thrown with a sling to a distance of 180 m.

FROMBOLIERE

It represents a bald Silenus who twists his mouth in a smile: it has a forehead furrowed with wrinkles, a drooping moustache and a bushy beard. On the upper part you can see a hole for hanging it.

A Silenus was a Genius of the water and he had a diving power.

This kind of object was used as a good luck talisman.

Room no, 6 - «Eugenio Cavallaro». The temple of Olympian Zeus.

The great figure standing up against the pilaster engaged in the eastern wall of the staircase

is the only one left of 38 figures that the architect of this temple had created for supporting the huge trabeation of the temple together with the columns.

It is a telamone, a giant male figure 7.61 m. tall that represents Atlas, the giant son of Jupiter and Asia who was condemned by Jupiter to support the world on his shoulders for having helped the Titans. It symbolized the rough power of nature that was subdued by Jupiter. The telamones that consist of 26 sandstone blocks and which were used both as supporting and decorative characters are fascinating and are still subjects under discussion.

Diodorus records that the decoration on the east side of the temple represented the battle of the Giants while on the West it represented the war of Troy.

On the northern side of the room you can see inside three niches heads of telamones with their hair arranged in waves which are the masterpieces that focus everybody's attention.

In the middle of the room you can see an exhibition of the different original hypothesis made about the building of the temple of Olympian Jupiter about which unfortunately there is no description of, in the field of Doric architecture.

With regard to the way the telamones were placed and to the reconstruction of the temple, this book mentions Pr. Anselmo Prado's hypothesis.

Room no, 7 - «Giulio Schubring». The layout of the ancient town (cases no, 66-72).

The layout of the ancient town (cases n. 66-72).

In this room there is an exhibition of the findings from the Hellenistic and Roman quarter that cover 1,000 years (from the 6th C. B.C. to the 4th C. A.D.). Houses are built on a large rectangular area of about 7,700 mq. and are arranged in a grid plan which took the name of the town planner Hippodamus from Mileto.

This town plan is one of the most interesting remains of the town of Agrigento which reached and surpassed the fame that many towns of the mother land had enjoyed for a long time. A main road (a decumanus) which is 10 m. wide, crosses longitudinally from the East towards the West the quarter; it is cut from the North to the South by four parallel roads (cardines) which are 5 m. wide. Those streets define the diffe-

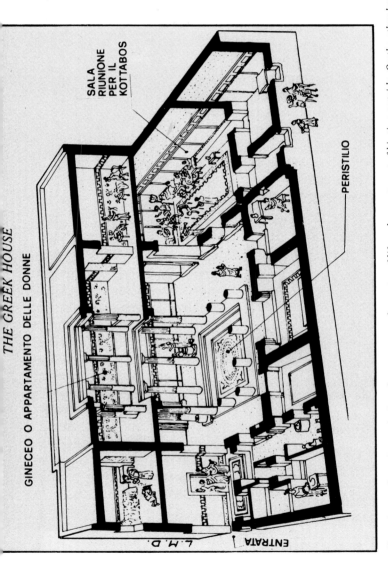

THE GREEK HOUSE

GINECEO O APPARTAMENTO DELLE DONNE

SALA RIUNIONE PER IL KOTTABOS

PERISTILIO

ENTRATA

L.M.D.

From the greek man's standpoint a house was not the centre of life as he spent most of his time outside. On the other hand his wife stayed almost always at home. A greek house consisted of the atrium (the servants' section) and the peristile (the owners' living rooms and reception rooms). In the triclinia rooms that usually contained three triclinai the table-companions laid on that were standing along three sides of the room thus leaving the third side free for the service, the guest with their left arm on a pillow used to eat with the fingers of their right hand. At the end of the IVth C. a house with garden costed 1,200 dracmae and could produce a rental revenue of 8%. A drachma consisted of 6 oboli that is an architect's daily wage. Usually rental contracts lasted for ten years.

rent blocks of parallel houses which are all the same size. The whole area covered with houses is 6,034 mq.. According to Cal-za, as a person can live in a 26 mq. area, in the quarter there lived at the most 232 people.

A slide exhibited right behind

the entrance and first of all a planimetric model hung on the facing wall, show the hippodameic plan.

The different archeological levels hung on the southern wall were excavated in 1961 in the house with the cryptoporticus. They show remains from both the Greek and the Roman town.

On the southern wall you can see fragments of Roman stuccos decorated in different colours with the encaustic technique (2nd style).

The emblematas

The emblematas hanging on the long wall of the room catch one's attention:

A gazelle at the spring. The floor figure representing a gazelle at a spring is a very fine masterwork. The animal is the centre piece of the scene of this mosaic which looks like a framed picture. The light and agile body depicted with realism and the nice landscape around make this gazelle pretty.

The house of the rooster. In the middle there is the so called mosaic of the « house of the rooster » which represents a rooster with a symbol of Hermes that is a money bag.

The house of the pheasant. The mosaic of the « house of the pheasant » ends the exhibition of mosaics in this room.

Room no, 8 - « Gaetano and Mario Columba »

In this room you can see an exhibition of Greek and Roman inscriptions:

- *the roman inscription « concordiae agrigentinorum »* which became famous for having given the name to the most beautiful and perfect Doric temple: the Temple of Concord. It is the text dating from the 2nd C. A.D. of a dedication made by the citizens of Lilibeo (today's Marsala) to the « concordia Agrigentinorum sacrum repubblica lilybetanorum dedicantibus M. Haterio Candido Proconsole et L. Cornelio Marcello Questore Propretore ».

Room no, 9 - « Antonio Salinas ». Coins (a special permit is needed for visiting it).

Nine show cases contain a rare collection of gold, silver and bronze coins. These coins date from the Greek, the Roman, the

L'EFEBO

Carthaginian, the Bizantine, the Arab and the Norman time. The Syracuse tetradachm dating from 480-479 B.C. is unique for its beauty. It was minted for celebrating the victory of Gelon the 1st and of Theron in Himera (today's Termini Imerese). There is a very nice Agrigento tetradrachm that was minted between 472 and 413 B.C. which shows a crab on obverse and an eagle on its reverse that is the coin symbols of the town.

Room no, 10 - « Valerio Villareale ». Greek and Roman sculpture (case no, 73).

The Agrigentan Ephebus: this outstanding small naked figure standing on a pedestal is a clean-cut sculpture representing a kouros dating from 480 B.C. that symbolizes the Greek ideal male beauty.

The kouros did not represent someone in particular but the ideal noble youth devote to God. They used to stand in the temples and they had raised hand for holding the offerings made to the Gods.

This statue was found in a cistern to the South of the temple of Demeter. It is 1 m. tall and has 35 cm. wide shoulders.

Crouched Aphrodite

Completely naked Aphrodite, the Goddes of beauty, was the most favourite subject of Praxiteles. Its wonderfully proportioned body was sculptured

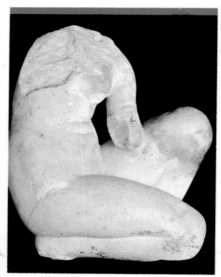

in a harmonious style. It represents the naked Goddess while she is going to bathe to regain her virginity. The complete nakedness of the Goddess propitiates fertility.

A male marble torso.
This torso which is 34.5 cm. tall is a very fine Greek sculpture. This masterwork which lacks the head, the forelimbs and the whole part under the hips is made in the classical style which was still followed in the

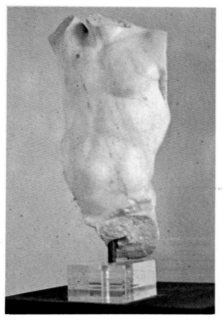

the monumental complexes have in the political organization of the Agrigentian polis.

The Ekklesiasterion and the Bouleuterion, rispectively to the south and north of the museum (capacity: 3000 people the first; 350 the second), gave life to the Doric constitutional model, adopted by Agrigento and characterized by great simplicity: the 'gerousia', that is, the senate, (which was called 'Synedrion' and later 'Bulè' in

2nd C. B.C.: this is probably the time it dates from.

On leaving the first wing of the L shaped hall, one enters the V bis Hall dedicated to Agrigento's civil and public buildings. We shall leave the description of the buildings where the individualization of a second agorà took place, (upstairs in the public area) situated in the zone of saint Nicola's mound, to the didactic apparatus on the wall, underlining the importance that

Agrigento), together with the king and the ephors, formed the supreme authority of the state, that controlled the administration and supervised everything, from the precise application of the law to the customs and supervised everything, from the pecise applications of the law to the customs and usances of the people. The kings were only "primi inter pares", first among equals, and were able to take their seat on the throne by direct succession of first born male heirs. Every month, before the ephors, they were obliged to renew their oaths to loyally obey the laws, whilst their judicial authority was limited to the controversies of domestic rights. The 'geronti' or elder senators, who in Agrigento were called 'Pritani', at the same time, both limited and coordinated, the kings' actions. They were elected verbally, for life, by a people's assembly, that is, the 'Apella', of which only the richer and more virtuous citizens, over the age of 60, took part. The five ephors, or supervisors, whose job it was to watch over the public and private life of the citizens, were elected by the assembly (one for each Doric tribe).

The chosen ones were all vastly competent men, chosen by the assembly for the job of preventing any kind change in the political structure of the country. They watched over the state's finances and taxes and duties, and moreover, sum-moned and presided over the popular assembly. The ephor's power lasted one year, at the end of which, the people were given a full account of their administration (docimasia).

The Ekklesia included all citizens who were over thirty years of age. The king, or rather the College of Ephors, presided over it and were usually convoked every month when there was a full moon.

In the showcase on the wall, in the centre, one can admire the marble base of a votive monument from the age of Augustea. The report is interesting because it shows that the city celebrated 'Imperial adoration', that is, the divinization of the Emperor Augusto, who encouraged the people of the earth to identify him as the saviour and protector of the world.

The period dominated by Augustus was called "Saeculum Augustum", an age of prosperity and peace.

Sventonio refers that Augusto boasted of having found a Rome made of brick and of having left a Rome made of marble.

Room no, 11 - « Raffaello Politi ». The Necropolis Findings (cases no, 74-84).

In this room which is dedicated to the necropolis of ancient Agrigento (from the archaic to the Byzantine period), there are many very fine finds. This is why only few of them will be described in this book.

In the big city of the dead, the funerary ceremony was mainly burial. However, several cases of cremation that is of burned persons were found, too.

The most important finds are:

1) *A soft white stone sarcophagus shaped like a bath tab* (228 cm. by 92.5 cm. by 90 cm.) which dates from about the 5th century.

3) *A marble sarcophagus shaped like a case with a Doric frieze* that dates from about the 5th C. B.C. and which was found in 1885 in the necropolis of Mon-

telusa. This masterwork shows Doric architectural decoration which surrounds it. The proportions are better respected on the longer sides than on the shorter ones (237 cm. by 95 cm. by 66 cm.). The frieze consists of horizontal and vertical features that represent the upper part of the trabeation of the Doric temple which was characterized by grooves and smooth rectangles that is the « trigliphs » and the « metopes ».

4) *A sarcophagus shaped like a case* (224 cm. by 72 cm.)

which dates from about the 2nd half of the 5th C. B.C.. It is a marble funerary case with acroterions at the corners and a sloping cover that was recently found in the necropolis Montelusa (in 1980). The decoration consists of a frieze representing meanders that serround the upper part of the sarcophagus just under the cover. Under it there is an ionic himation motif, that is the lotus flower that propitiates resurrection in the underworld, while its red colour protects and set the dead free from evil eye. Until short time ago red colour was used in weddings: arab brides painted their nails red and were covered with a red veil in order to protect them and to keep evil eye that was always feared in eastern countries, away from them. Inside the sarcophagus there are still the remains of a woman, all

the objects accompanying her and the funeral meal that consisted of several different kinds of grains.

5) *The roman sarcophagus shaped like a case of the dying child with decorations representing the child playing, studying and having the holy bath.*

This very interesting masterwork was found by chance in 1973 to the South of the temple of Hercules.

This sarcophagus represents four scenes of family life concerning the dead: his playing time, his education, his death and his holy bath. On the left representing the child sitting on a waggon drown by a ram. He looks busy but at the same time he is enjoying it. On the front side (92 cm. long and 40 cm. high) 18 figures compose two different scenes: the child who is repeating the lesson and the child who is dying. Surely the most complicated part is the « conclamation scene » that is calling the dead's name three times. The most realistic charcter that can be seen in this scene is that of the bearded grand father: he is bald and is sitting bent over on a chair. He is looking at the floor and it seems like he would refuse to talk even

short side (44 cm. long and 40 cm. high) you can see a scene if he could. He is breathless. The grand mother bent over on a chair and with her head covered with a cloak has an imploring expression. She is praying and invoking a diagnosis of recovery. But the most touching figure is that of the mother: grief and desperation can be seen on the face of the mother who expresses them by putting her hands up, too. The father who has the most interesting face of the whole masterwork is calling the name of his child. The figure shows a deep inside balance and important power over the other characters. It is a well proportioned figure. He is bald on the upper part of his head and his beard is still bushy. He is the one who has to call the name of his son («conclamatio») while putting his arms up before declaring him as dead. On the other short side (44 cm. long and 40 cm. high) there is depicted the scene of the whole family consisting of 7 people who have gathered for the holy bath. The bath represents the respect that the child has for the Gods of the Underworld by showing himself in his dignity in order to make friends. The child who is completely naked is very nice to see. His figure is perfect. He is going to get the holy bath and he looks like he is ready to enjoy the liquid over him. The ball on the column-shaped altar symbolizes the dedication to the Gods of the child's toy thus representing the deep value of memory moved to the holy field. This was a common habit of both Greek and Roman young people. As matter of fact when they became adolescent, they used to offer the Gods all their toys.

This masterwork dates from about the end of the 1st C. and the 2nd C. A.D..

6) *A bath-tub shaped sarcophagus made of soft stone* (20 cm. by 74.5 cm. by 46.5 cm.).

It dates from about the 4th C. A.D. It used to belong to the Monastery of Santo Spirito.

This masterwork which has a rectangular shape is interesting for the precise lines of the dead man's portrait and of the medallion. The composotion is devide in two parts and shows under the medallion two fighting roosters; on the left you can see a billy goat. Along the sides two simmetrical groups representing Eros and Psyche symbolize the

dead man's happy married life: a marriage in order to be happy needs not only physical beauty but also the soul one.

7) *A strigilate marble slab.*
On the facing wall you can see a marble slab which was used for closing a tomb (16.8 cm. high and 80 cm. long). The portrait shows the dead who wanted to be remebered as pro-

fessional drama actor. His wife is holding his arm with her hand thus expressing in a touching way her sorrow for their separation and her resignation to the inevitable. It is a compo-

sition which gives those simple figures an eternal character.

A bronze crater with spiralled handles.

The bronze, spiralled crater in the form of a swan's head is 55.5 centimetres high and dates back to the end of the V century B.C., it was found in the necropolis of Mosé. A woman's funeral outfit, including two delikè (water jugs) with ginecèo and toilet (dressing table) scenes; an alabasuno (an object that held the perfumed oil used for massages); a kilix (a drinking cup), a jug and some wood fragments, probably from a comb.

Room no, 12 - « Paolo Orsi ».
Prehistory of Agrigento district.

This room shows the most

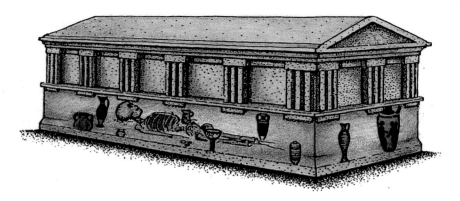

Reconstruction by Hendrike Schoof

ancient manifestation of human activity from Paleolithic onwards that is to Aeneolithic, to Bronze Age and to Iron Age. You can see amygdalas (primitive armaments shaped like almonds), clay pottery. fibulas, pendants, fuseroles and snails' shells.

The illuminated panels hunging on the right wall show an educational exhibition of the collections that can be easily understood by the visitors and can be appreciated even by those who are not particularly concerned with prehistory.

In the first two cases of the room there are finds that come from the top of Hill Cozzo Busonè. This was an ancient religious site used from early Aeneolithic (2800 C. B.C.). The importance of these objects is due mainly to the fact that little is known about the Aeneolithic Age, of the district. On one hand there are well knowm objects such as the axe, the scraper, the millstone, the pastel, that were found on the whole island; on the other hand there

are little known objects such as the stonepillow covered with red ocre and the « Veneri del Pozzetto », which are the only realistic prehistorical characters found in Agrigento. The « Veneri (Venuses) » are the best re-

ligious evidence connected to the Goddess of Fertility who was later called Demeter, the great Goddess of the ground and of corn. They represent a spindle-shaped figure and you can notice the artist's effort to make the schematic lines on the body more natural.

Again from Castellana's excavations:

A beautiful example of a small, round-shaped temple in terracotta, (15,7 cm. in height and 16,3 in diameter) made by curving and joining the four winged pillars, with the winged

support in the centre. Professor Castellana interprets the scene as a ritual dance with four idols forming a circle around the central idol. In the same showcase one can admire a basin, a flat-based pan, a globe-shaped orciolo and auaste the 'orciolo' is a small vase used for containing an 'orciolo' is a small uase pouring liquids and a vase.

Room no, 13 - « Umberto Zanotti Bianco ». Prehistory of Agrigento district (cases no, 89-102).

These stone and clay finds have to be considered as precious evidence and as symbols of an important technical development which sometimes took place very slowly and hence is hard to be caught in its different stages. This is why besides being examples of prehistorical art that in some cases have artistic value, they are special souvenirs of the past. The collection of epigravethian stone implements is very important.

Case no, 89

It is dedicated to the epigravethian stone production.

It is a rich collection of stone implements exhibited according o the different shapes and to what they were used for.

Their names depend on what they were used for: burins were used for cutting and carving bones and wood; scrapers for skins and wood; blades for cutting; saw-toothed tools were used for sawing and mowing; blunted-back points were used for cutting holes in the skins; blunted-back blades were used as knives.

Case no, 93

There is a nice bell-shaped vase decorated with deeply carved parallel lines that had to contain according to Bray and Trump an alcoholic drink for the last trip of the dead.

Case no, 99

A nice fruit bowl with 7 pierced small handles and a tubular pedestal, stands out for quality of style. This is a great shining specimen made on a wheel.

Room no, 14 - « Giulio Emanuele Rizzo ». (Cases no, 103-119).

Our knowledge about the presence of Greek, Roman and Byzantine remains in the district of Agrigento is based on finds that come from archeological sites where excavations have been carried out.

Thanks to those intense and precise digs that were made in the archeological sites of Agrigento, it has been possible to arrange step by step the 17 cases of this room that give a historical and cultural view of a district which has revealed a great archeological richness.

In particular this room is rich of finds that point out in several different ways life in the ancient Agrigento district.

In the cases you can see:

Case no, 104 (from tomb A)

A little clay mouse

This little mouse-shaped vase is not only a decorative object but it was used both for practical and religious purposes. This object which could be hung and that has a thin beak for pouring, was made to con-

tain honey medecines that were used as last remedies for children's deseases.

Mice symbolized deseases and treatments. That is why the Greeks venerated Apollo Smintheus as God of medeci-

ne (the word « smintheus » that has Cretan origins means « mouse »).

In the temple of Apollo white mice bred freely in order to fight mice invasions and plagues hat occurred very often at that time.

An alabaster ointment jar (from tomb E22).

This object was an ointment jar that contained the perfumed oil that was used for making massages after bath; it was carried by means of a small rope tied up around one's wrist.

A herma of Pan found in Caltabellotta surroundings.

In this case you can see a nice head of Pan, the God of shepherds, of hunters, of animals and of woods.

It is a marble masterwork that dates from the Roman time and that represents the God with straggling hair, snub nose, pointed beard. Unfortunately, its goat's horns are damaged. According to some people, Pan (that in Greek means « everything ») represents everything: with his horns he represents the sun and the moon, with his chubby face the air, with his thick hair the trees and the animals, with his goat's foot the firmness of the Earth. The Lupecalia feasts that is feasts of purification were made in his honour every year on February the 15th. After the banquet during which goats and dogs were sacrificed, the Luperci (that is those who kept the wolves away) ran in the streets while holding strips of the sacrificed goats that they met. Women without children wanted sto be hit by the Luperci as that was thought to propritiate fertility.

Agricultural iron implements. The ancients used to use several different agricultural implements. In this case you can see a plough the most important of which was the plough-share, a hoe, a spook, an axe, two bill-hooks for the vines. It must be noticed that most of these typical agricultural implements still show the same shape they had in the past.

It can be interesting to know that the desease that affected the vine Metana was treated in the following way: a rooster was cut in two and a couple of men turned around the vineyard while holding one half of it each; in the same spot where they met, the remains of the animal were buried as it was thought that they had negative impurities that affected the vine. In Tanagra, an ephebus used to carry a lamb, on his shoulders around the vine in order to prevent deseases. In other towns the evil eye was averted by making a procession through the vineyard that was lead by either a menstruating naked girl or woman.

Room no, 15 - « Carlo and Cesare Navarra ». Gela (case no, 120).

The vase of Gela. An elegant red-figure crater with volute shaped handles is 78 cm. high and dates from about 460 B.C..

127

It is exhibited in the middle of the room that is the right place for showing such perfect masterpiece. It is surely a great piece of the Agrigento vase collection which has a value of one billion liras and that is attributed to the Niobid Painter.

The Centauromachia is admirable: along the neck, just under the palmettes, it represents the episode concerning Herakles and Pholo. Herakles met him during the expedition against the wildboar of Erimantho. Pholo, who was kind and friendly, made him the meal and then he was convinced to open an amphora of special wine belonging to all Centaurs who lived on Mount Pholos. As soon as they smellt the wine they came down galloping umbridled and armed with rocks and trunks of trees. Herakles made them escape by throwing firebrands against them and killed some of them with his arrows; the others escaped towards Maldea Cape.

Along the body you can see represented the fight between the Greeks and the Amazons and the episode concerning Hyppolyta and Theseus who is holding a rounded shield with his left hand and has just siesed Hyppolita's right arm who is fighting against him. According to tradition Hyppolyta gave him a child who was called Hyppolytus like his mother. He inspired a myth which is depicted on the famous sarcophagus of Phoedra which can be seen in the second chapel of the near Church of San Nicola.

On the back of the vase you can see represented Pentiselea, another Queen of the Amazons who rushed to the Troyans' help. The scene shows Achilles who becomes infatuated with Pentiselea right at the same time he hits her mortally. This episode is very wise: proud and invincible Achilles is only a plaything subjected to destiny.

Room no, 16 - « Luigi Preti » (under preparation).

Room no, 17 - « Giulio Libertini ». Caltanissetta district (cases no, 121-140).

According to the large number of alabaster ointment jars (42), of strigils, of mirrors and of parfum jars only one of which is made of glass paste, that were found in the area of Vassallaggi near San Cataldo, it seems that this Greek and Sican site had to be like Paris today. Yo can see:

Case no, 121 - 2nd shelf

A hinged doll (inv. 9467)

This very small example of clay hinged doll is similar to Dedalus' one that the famous Athenian architect had made in order to delight Minos' daugh-

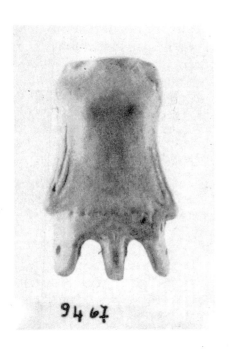

94 6⊥

gil that can be seen in this case.

Case no, 126 (inv. 1852)

ters. It symbolized Ariadne (fertility), The Goddess of fertility and wife of Dionysius. It used to be hung on a fruit tree, in the middle of the garden, where by spinning because of the wind, it fertilized the spots of the field reached by the mind. On the famous golden ring of the Acropolys of Mycenae you can see one of those dolls hanging from a fruit tree.

The strigil.

It is an « S » shaped bronze tool. Before starting gymnastic or wrestling, the Greek boys used to cover their body with very fine sand. After wrestling they used to scrape themselves with the bronze tool called stri-

An important find is the surgical knife. It is a blunt-back knife which is still covered with a veil.

A woman's skull with remains of hair and a gold plated bronze hair-band.

Obviously one's attention is caught by the woman's skull with remanins of hair and a gold plated bronze hair band that dates from the 5th C. B.C. The bronze hair-band was used in order to point out the beauty of the body.

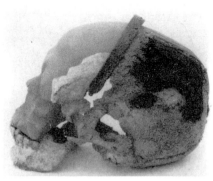

A bronze mirror (inv. 2327).

Mirrors were very much required by the Greek women and girls and they were always included in the make-up set of all well-to-do women.

A missile-shaped tomb of child (inv. 155).

It is very interesting to see this tomb for a child inside which there are several clay figurines of animals that were used as toys and rattles.

Rattles and castanets were very much used in the ancient time (and still are by primitive communities) in order to drive out the demons of fever.

Artemis was the Goddess who could cause and treat fever thanks to her miraculous arrows.

Case no, 137

A Siren.

The Siren which is represented with head of woman and body of bird is interesting because of what it represented. She was a Goddess of death who personified fever. She was associated with the worship of Artemis who could provoke or treat fever with her miracolous arrows. It is thought that Sirens lived on the island of Sirens near Paestum or Capri. They sang so sweetly that they attracted sailors to the fields of their island where the bones of their previous victims were piled up. As it was believed that the soul flew away in the shape of a bird, they were described as the Arpies like birds ready to catch their prey.

The birthplace of Luigi Pirandello

At 6 kilometres from Agrigento, in the vicinity of Porto Empedocle, in the zone of Caos, is the rural birthplace of Luigi Pirandello (1867-1936), Nobel prize for literature, whose ashes are preserved in a burial niche at the foot of a pine tree overlooking the sea. He was born on June 28th 1867, in a cottage in the district of Caos, in the borough of Agrigento. The family had moved there because of a cholera epidemic which had raged over Agrigento. After finishing his initial studies at Agrigento, Palermo and Rome, he took a degree at Bonn in 1891. In 1894 he married Antonietta Portulano at Agrigento and between 1895 and 1899 they had three children: Stefano, Lietta and Fausto. In 1908 he was sent for to teach "Italian language, stylistics and precepts, and the study of the classics including Greek and Latin" at the Superior Institute of Magistery of Rome, The literary merits of Pirandello were 'crowned in 1929 with the honour of Accademic of Italy and in 1934 with the Nobel prize for literature.

Luigi Pirandello died in Rome on December 12th 1936. The attic crater which contains the writer's ashes is preserved in the archeological Museum of Agrigento. The ashes were gathered by his son Stephen and brought from Rome to Agrigento, as his father had wanted. The Pirandellian production is extremely vast and concerns essayistic, the fiction of the theatre. We quote the titles of his more complete works: "Short Stories for a year", "All novels", Nude Masks", "Poems", "Essays". In Pirandello's house, a national monument since 1949, one can find interesting memoirs, photographs and school report showing bad marks for Italian language.

INDEX